PRACTICE - ASSESS - DIAGNOSE

180 Days of SCIENCE for Kindergarten

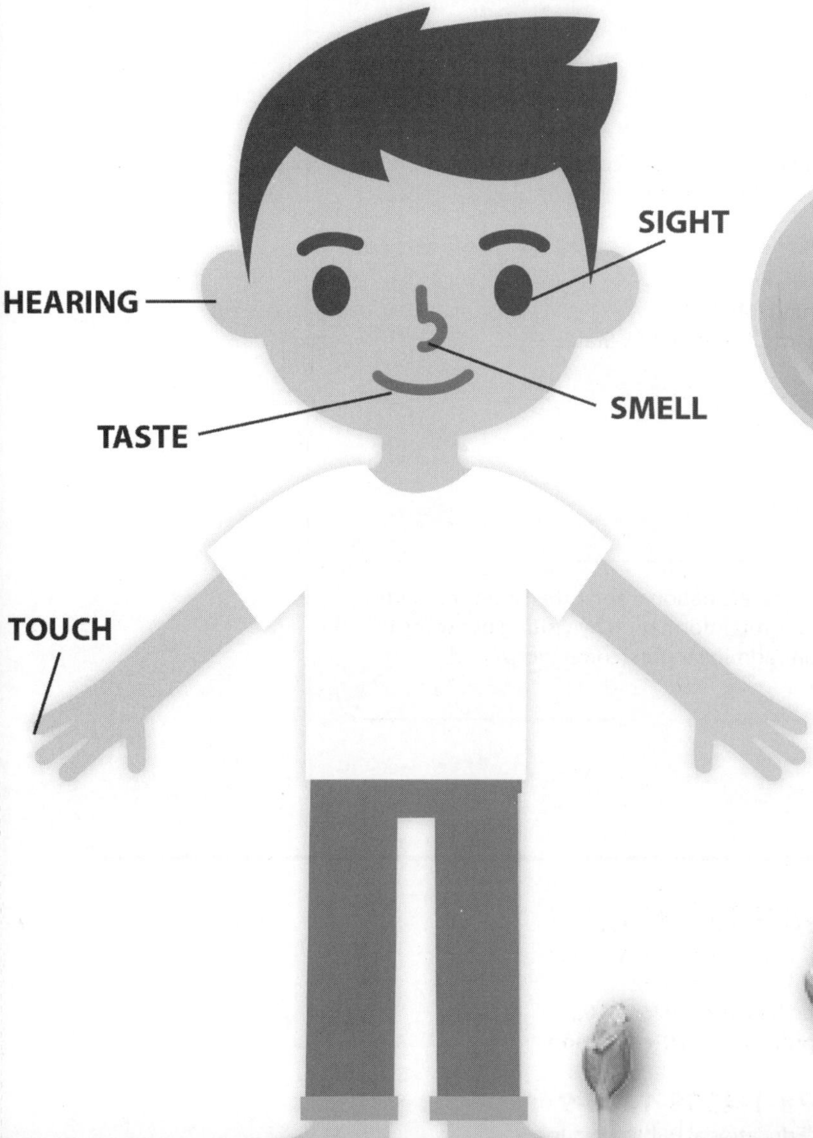

Author
Lauren Homayoun

SHELL EDUCATION

Earth & Space
Life
Physical

Publishing Credits

Corinne Burton, M.A.Ed., *Publisher*
Conni Medina, M.A.Ed., *Managing Editor*
Emily R. Smith, M.A.Ed., *Content Director*
Shaun Bernadou, *Art Director*
Lynette Ordoñez, *Editor*

Image Credits

p. 100 Ivan Kurmyshov/Shutterstock.com; p. 136 Mai Groves/Shutterstock.com; p. 160 teeflow/Shutterstock.com; p. 190 Paolo Bona/Shutterstock.com; all other images from iStock and/or Shutterstock.

Standards

© 2014 Mid-continent Research for Education and Learning (McREL)
NGSS Lead States. 2013. Next Generation Science Standards: For States, By States. Washington, DC: The National Academies Press.

For information on how this resource meets national and other state standards, see pages 10–13. You may also review this information by visiting our website at www.teachercreatedmaterials.com/administrators/correlations/ and following the on-screen directions.

Shell Education
A division of Teacher Created Materials
5301 Oceanus Drive
Huntington Beach, CA 92649-1030
www.tcmpub.com/shell-education

ISBN 978-1-4258-1406-9

Printed by: 584728
Printed in: India
PO#: 24284

Table of Contents

Introduction

With today's science and technology, there are more resources than ever to help students understand how the world works. Information about science experiments you can do at home is widely available online. Many students have experience with physics concepts from games.

While students may be familiar with many of the topics discussed in this book, it is not uncommon for them to have misconceptions about certain subjects. It is important for students to learn how to apply scientific practices in a classroom setting and within their lives.

Science is the study of the physical and natural world through observation and experiment. Not only is it important for students to learn scientific facts, but it is important for them to develop a thirst for knowledge. This leads to students who are anxious to learn and who understand how to follow practices that will lead them to the answers they seek.

The Need for Practice

To be successful in science, students must understand how people interact with the physical world. They must not only master scientific practices but also learn how to look at the world with curiosity. Through repeated practice, students will learn how a variety of factors affect the world in which they live.

Understanding Assessment

In addition to providing opportunities for frequent practice, teachers must be able to assess students' scientific understandings. This allows teachers to adequately address students' misconceptions, build on their current understandings, and challenge them appropriately. Assessment is a long-term process that involves careful analysis of student responses from discussions, projects, or practice sheets. The data gathered from assessments should be used to inform instruction: slow down, speed up, or reteach. This type of assessment is called *formative assessment.*

How to Use This Book

Weekly Structure

All 36 weeks of this book follow a regular weekly structure. The book is divided into three sections: Life Science, Physical Science, and Earth and Space Science. The book is structured to give students a strong foundation on which to build throughout the year. It is also designed to adequately prepare them for state standardized tests.

Each week focuses on one topic. Day 1 sets the stage by providing background information on the topic that students will need throughout the week. In Day 2, students analyze data related to the topic. Day 3 leads students through developing scientific questions. Day 4 guides students through planning a solution. Finally, Day 5 helps students communicate results from observations or investigations.

Day 1—Learning Content: Students will read grade-appropriate content and answer questions about it.

Day 2—Analyzing Data: Students will analyze scientific data and answer questions about it.

Day 3—Developing Questions: Students will read a scenario related to the topic, answer questions, and formulate a scientific question about the information.

Day 4—Planning Solutions: Students will read a scenario related to the topic, answer questions, and develop a solution or plan an investigation.

Day 5—Communicating Results: Students accurately communicate the results of an investigation or demonstrate what they learned throughout the week.

Three Strands of Science

This book allows students to explore the three strands of science: life science, physical science, and earth and space science. Life science teaches students about the amazing living things on our planet and how they interact in ecosystems. Physical science introduces students to physics and chemistry concepts that will lay the groundwork for deeper understanding later in their education. Earth and space science familiarizes students with the wonders of the cosmos and the relationships between the sun, Earth, moon, and stars.

How to Use This Book *(cont.)*

Weekly Topics

The following chart shows the weekly focus topics that are covered during each week of instruction.

Unit	Week	Science Topic
Life Science	1	Living Things
	2	Plants and Animals
	3	The Human Body
	4	Animal Bodies
	5	Plant Parts
	6	Flowers
	7	Bees and Other Bugs
	8	Animal Habitats
	9	Homes and Habitats
	10	Baby Animals
	11	Seeds to Sprouts
	12	Healthy Living
Physical Science	1	What Things Are Made Of
	2	Light or Heavy?
	3	How Things Move
	4	Gravity
	5	Magnets in Motion
	6	Sight
	7	Sound
	8	Smell
	9	Taste
	10	Touch
	11	Solid, Liquid, Gas
	12	Science Tools
Earth and Space Science	1	Weather Patterns
	2	Seasonal Changes
	3	Winter Wonders
	4	Spring Things
	5	Sizzling Summer
	6	Fall Features
	7	Land, Water, Air
	8	Deserts, Tundras, and Savannas
	9	From Rainforests to Oceans
	10	The Sun, Moon, and Stars
	11	Earth
	12	Taking Care of Earth

How to Use This Book *(cont.)*

Best Practices for This Series

- Use the practice pages to introduce important science topics to your students.
- Use the Weekly Topics chart on page 5 to align the content to what you're covering in class. Then, treat the pages in this book as jumping off points for that content.
- Use the practice pages as formative assessment of the science strands and key topics.
- Use the weekly themes to engage students in content that is new to them.
- Read the text passages aloud to students.
- Lead teacher-directed discussions of the vocabulary and concepts presented in some of the more complex weeks.
- Support students in practicing the varied types of questions asked throughout the practice pages.
- When possible, have students participate in hands-on activities to answer the questions they generate and do the investigations they plan.

Using the Resources

An answer key for all days can be found on pages 194–200. Rubrics for Day 3 (developing questions), Day 4 (planning solutions), and Day 5 (communicating results) can be found on pages 202–204 and in the Digital Resources. Use the answer keys and rubrics to assess students' work. Be sure to share these rubrics with students so that they know what is expected of them.

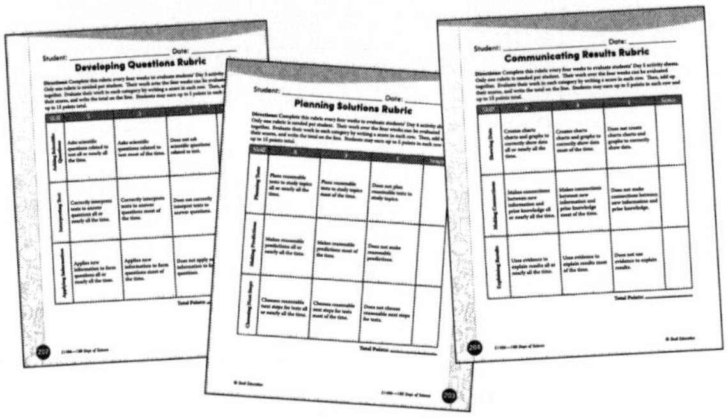

How to Use This Book *(cont.)*

Diagnostic Assessment

Teachers can use the practice pages as diagnostic assessments. The data analysis tools included with the book enable teachers or parents to quickly score students' work and monitor their progress. Teachers and parents can see which skills students may need to target further to develop proficiency.

Students will learn science content, how to analyze data, how to develop scientific questions, how to plan solutions, and how to accurately communicate results. You can assess students' learning using the answer key for all days. Rubrics are also provided on pages 202–204 for Days 3–5 to help you further assess key analytical skills that are needed for success with the scientific practices. Then, record their scores on the Practice Page Item Analysis sheets (pages 205–207). These charts are provided as PDFs, Microsoft Word® files, and Microsoft Excel® files. Teachers can input data into the electronic files directly, or they can print the pages.

To Complete the Practice Page Analysis Charts

- Write or type students' names in the far-left column. Depending on the number of students, more than one copy of the form may be needed or you may need to add rows.
    - The science strands are indicated across the tops of the charts.
    - Students should be assessed every four weeks, as indicated in the first rows of the charts.
- For each student, evaluate his or her work over the past four weeks using the answer key for Days 1 and 2 and the rubrics for Days 3–5.
- Review students' work for the weeks indicated in the chart. For example, if using the *Life Science Analysis Chart* for the first time, review students' work from weeks 1–4. Add the scores for Days 1 and 2 for each student, and record those in the appropriate columns. Then, write students' rubric scores for Days 3–5 in the corresponding columns. Use these scores as benchmarks to determine how each student is performing.

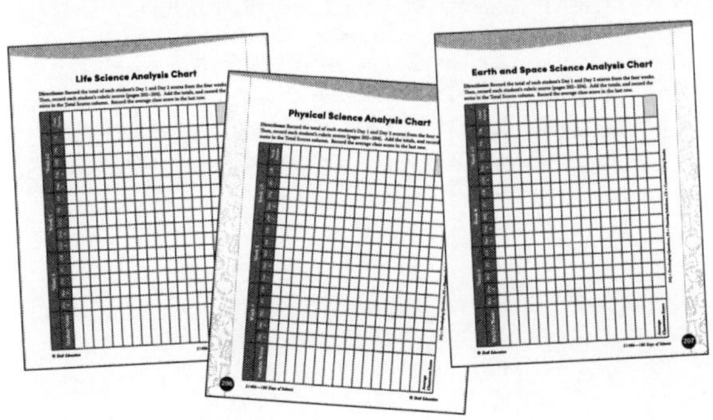

Digital Resources

The Digital Resources contain digital copies of the rubrics, analysis sheets, and standards correlations. See page 208 for more information.

How to Use This Book *(cont.)*

Using the Results to Differentiate Instruction

Once results are gathered and analyzed, teachers can use the results to inform the way they differentiate instruction. The data can help determine which science skills and topics are the most difficult for students and which students need additional instructional support and continued practice.

Whole-Class Support

The results of the diagnostic analysis may show that the entire class is struggling with certain science topics. If these concepts have been taught in the past, this indicates that further instruction or reteaching is necessary. If these concepts have not been taught in the past, this data is a great preassessment and may demonstrate that students do not have a working knowledge of the concepts. Thus, careful planning for the length of the unit(s) or lesson(s) must be considered, and additional front-loading may be required.

Small-Group or Individual Support

The results of the diagnostic analysis may show that an individual student or a small group of students is struggling with certain science skills. If these concepts have been taught in the past, this indicates that further instruction or reteaching is necessary. Consider pulling these students aside to instruct them further on the concepts while others are working independently. Students may also benefit from extra practice using games or computer-based resources.

Teachers can also use the results to help identify proficient individual students or groups of students who are ready for enrichment or above-grade-level instruction. These students may benefit from independent learning contracts or more challenging activities.

Standards Correlations

Shell Education is committed to producing educational materials that are research and standards based. In this effort, we have correlated all of our products to the academic standards of all 50 states, the District of Columbia, the Department of Defense Dependents Schools, and all Canadian provinces.

How to Find Standards Correlations

To print a customized correlation report of this product for your state, visit our website at **www.teachercreatedmaterials.com/administrators/correlations/** and follow the on-screen directions. If you require assistance in printing correlation reports, please contact our Customer Service Department at 1-877-777-3450.

Purpose and Intent of Standards

The Every Student Succeeds Act (ESSA) mandates that all states adopt challenging academic standards that help students meet the goal of college and career readiness. While many states already adopted academic standards prior to ESSA, the act continues to hold states accountable for detailed and comprehensive standards.

Standards are designed to focus instruction and guide adoption of curricula. Standards are statements that describe the criteria necessary for students to meet specific academic goals. They define the knowledge, skills, and content students should acquire at each level. Standards are also used to develop standardized tests to evaluate students' academic progress. Teachers are required to demonstrate how their lessons meet state standards. State standards are used in the development of all of our products, so educators can be assured they meet the academic requirements of each state.

McREL Compendium

Each year, McREL analyzes state standards and revises the compendium to produce a general compilation of national standards. The standards listed on pages 10–11 support the objectives presented throughout the weeks.

Next Generation Science Standards

This set of national standards aims to incorporate knowledge and process standards into a cohesive framework. The standards listed on pages 12–13 support the objectives presented throughout the weeks.

Standards Correlations *(cont.)*

180 Days of Science is designed to give students daily practice in the three strands of science. The weeks support the McREL standards and NGSS performance expectations listed in the charts below.

McREL Standards		
Standard	**Weeks**	**Unit**
Understands that living things have similar needs.	1, 2	Life Science
Knows simple ways that living things can be grouped.	2	Life Science
Knows that plants and animals have features that help them live in different environments.	3–6	Life Science
Knows that plants and animals closely resemble their parents.	3–6	Life Science
Knows that differences exist among individuals of the same kind of plant or animal.	3–6	Life Science
Knows that there are similarities and differences in the appearance and behavior of plants and animals.	7	Life Science
Knows that living things are found almost everywhere in the world and that distinct environments support the life of different types of plants and animals.	8, 9	Life Science
Knows that living things go through a process of growth and change.	10, 11	Life Science
Knows the basic needs of plants and animals.	10, 11	Life Science
Knows that plants and animals need certain resources for energy and growth.	12	Life Science
Knows vocabulary used to describe some observable properties of objects.	1, 2	Physical Science
Knows that different objects are made up of many different types of materials and have many different observable properties.	1, 2	Physical Science
Knows that objects can be moved in space in a number of ways.	3	Physical Science
Knows the effects of forces in nature.	4	Physical Science
Knows that things near the Earth fall to the ground unless something holds them up.	4	Physical Science
Knows that magnets can be used to make some things move without being touched.	5	Physical Science

Standards Correlations *(cont.)*

McREL Standards		
Standard	**Weeks**	**Unit**
Uses the senses to make observations about living things, nonliving objects, and events.	6–10	Physical Science
Knows that Earth materials consist of solid rocks, soils, liquid water, and the gases of the atmosphere.	11	Physical Science
Uses simple tools to gather information.	12	Physical Science
Knows that tools can be used to gather information and extend the senses.	12	Physical Science
Knows vocabulary for different types of weather.	1	Earth and Space Science
Knows that weather conditions change over time.	1	Earth and Space Science
Knows how the environment changes over the seasons.	2–6	Earth and Space Science
Knows that short-term weather conditions can change daily, and weather patterns change over the seasons.	2–6	Earth and Space Science
Knows that there are different materials on Earth.	7, 11	Earth and Space Science
Knows properties of a number of Earth materials.	7, 11	Earth and Space Science
Knows that Earth materials consist of solid rocks, soils, liquid water, and the gases of the atmosphere.	7, 11	Earth and Space Science
Knows that living things are found almost everywhere in the world and that distinct environments support the life of different types of plants and animals.	8, 9	Earth and Space Science
Knows that there are different materials.	8, 9	Earth and Space Science
Knows vocabulary used to describe major features of the sky.	10, 11	Earth and Space Science
Knows basic patterns of the Sun and Moon.	10, 11	Earth and Space Science

Standards Correlations *(cont.)*

Next Generation Science Standards					
Unit	Week	Performance Expectation	Science and Engineering Practices	Disciplinary Core Ideas	Cross-Cutting Concepts
Life Science	1	Use observations to describe patterns of what plants and animals (including humans) need to survive.	Analyzing and Interpreting Data	Organization for Matter and Energy Flow in Organisms	Patterns
	2	Use a model to represent the relationship between the needs of different plants or animals (including humans) and the places they live.	Developing and Using Models	Natural Resources	Systems and System Models
	8	Use a model to represent the relationship between the needs of different plants or animals (including humans) and the places they live.	Developing and Using Models	Natural Resources	Systems and System Models
	9	Use a model to represent the relationship between the needs of different plants or animals (including humans) and the places they live.	Developing and Using Models	Natural Resources	Systems and System Models

Next Generation Science Standards					
Unit	Week	Performance Expectation	Science and Engineering Practices	Disciplinary Core Ideas	Cross-Cutting Concepts
Physical Science	3	Plan and conduct an investigation to compare the effects of different strengths or different directions of pushes and pulls on the motion of an object.	Planning and Carrying Out Investigations	Forces and Motion Types of Interactions	Cause and Effect
	4	Plan and conduct an investigation to compare the effects of different strengths or different directions of pushes and pulls on the motion of an object.	Planning and Carrying Out Investigations	Forces and Motion Types of Interactions	Cause and Effect

Standards Correlations *(cont.)*

Next Generation Science Standards					
Unit	Week	Performance Expectation	Science and Engineering Practices	Disciplinary Core Ideas	Cross-Cutting Concepts
Earth and Space Science	1	Use and share observations of local weather conditions to describe patterns over time.	Analyzing and Interpreting Data	Weather and Climate	Patterns
Earth and Space Science	12	Communicate solutions that will reduce the impact of humans on the land, water, air, and/or other living things in the local environment.	Obtaining, Evaluating, and Communicating Information	Human Impacts on Earth Systems	Cause and Effect

Name: ______________________ **Date:** ____________

Directions: Read the text. Answer the questions.

Living Things

Plants and animals are living things that grow. Plants need light to live and grow. Animals need food. Both need water. Some things aren't living. They don't need food or water.

1. What do **both** plants and animals need?

a. water

b. food

2. Do all living things grow?

a. yes **b.** no

Name: ______________________ Date: ____________

Directions: Look at the chart. Answer the questions.

It grows.	**X**		**X**
It needs water.	**X**		**X**
It does not need water.		**X**	

1. Which one is **not** a living thing?

a. rock 

b. dog 

2. Which one **is** a living thing?

a. flower 

b. rock 

Name: ______________________ **Date:** __________

Directions: Read the text. Answer the questions.

Jada puts a plant near a sunny window. She forgets to water it. The leaves turn brown. The leaves are dry. The plant is not healthy.

1. What color are healthy leaves?

a. brown

b. green

2. What does a plant need?

a. water

b. milk

3. Say a question Jada could have about healthy plants.

Name: ______________________ **Date:** ____________

Directions: Read the text. Answer the questions.

Plants need light to grow. Plants need water, too. Jada's plant is not growing. It gets lots of water. Sometimes Jada forgets to give it sunlight.

1. What can Jada do to help her plant grow?

a. Give it more water.

b. Give it more sunlight.

2. How can Jada remember to give her plant sunlight? Draw a picture that will help her remember.

Name: ______________________________ **Date:** ____________

Directions: Read the text. Answer the questions.

Dwayne gives his puppy wet food and dry food. He wants to know which food the puppy likes more. The puppy will eat the food he likes more first. The puppy eats the wet food first.

1. Which food did the puppy eat first?

2. Which food did the puppy like best?

Name: ______________________________ **Date:** ____________

Directions: Read the text. Answer the questions.

Plants and Animals

Plants and animals are alive. Plants start as seeds. Animals move from place to place. Plants stay in one place. Animals start as babies.

Animals

Plants

1. Which one is the animal?

a. bird

b. cactus

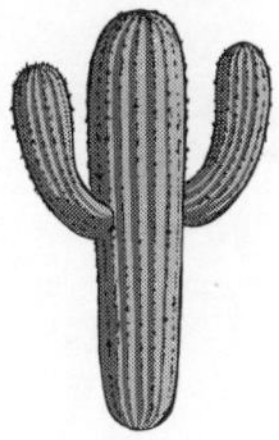

2. Which living thing stays in one place?

a. cactus

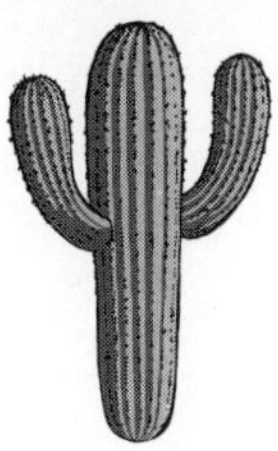

b. bird

Name: ______________________ **Date:** ____________

Directions: Look at the chart. Answer the questions.

Animals move.			**X**	**X**
Animals start as a babies.			**X**	**X**
Plants stay in one place.	**X**	**X**		
Plants start as seeds.	**X**	**X**		

1. What is a rabbit?

a. a plant

b. an animal

2. What is a tree?

a. a plant

b. an animal

Name: ______________________ **Date:** ____________

Directions: Read the text. Answer the questions.

Lou likes to play outside. He likes to look at the leaves on plants. He sees a black spot on a leaf. He looks at the spot. The spot flies away.

1. What did Lou see on the leaf?

   a. a black spot **b.** another leaf

2. Say a question Lou could ask about the leaf.

3. Say a question Lou could ask about the spot.

Name: ______________________ **Date:** __________

Directions: Read the text. Answer the questions.

Mona likes flowers. Mona wants to grow them in her garden. Mona needs seeds first. Flowers need water to grow.

1. What should Mona do first?

   a. buy seeds

   b. buy cutters

2. How can Mona make her flowers grow?

   a. She can plant seeds and give them water.

   b. She can plant seeds and put them in the shade.

Name: ______________________ **Date:** ____________

Directions: Jai watched two living things grow. Help him show his results.

1. A kitten grows into a cat. Trace the cat.

2. A seed grows into a plant. Draw the plant.

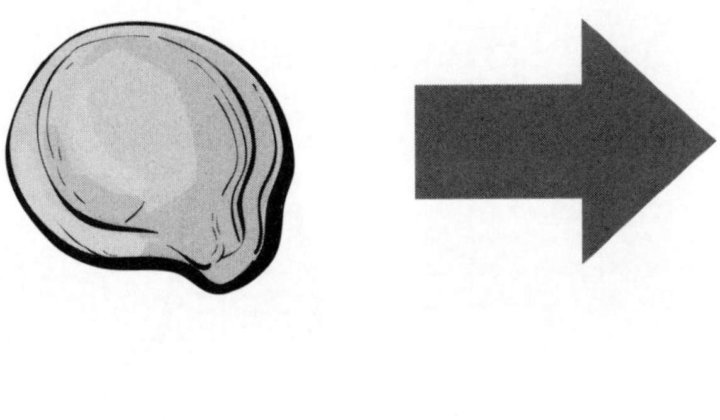

Name: ______________________ **Date:** __________

Directions: Read the text. Answer the questions.

The Human Body

Our bodies help us do many things. Our eyes help us see. Our ears help us hear. Our mouths help us taste. Our hands help us touch. Our noses help us smell.

1. Which body part helps you see?

a. eyes

b. hands

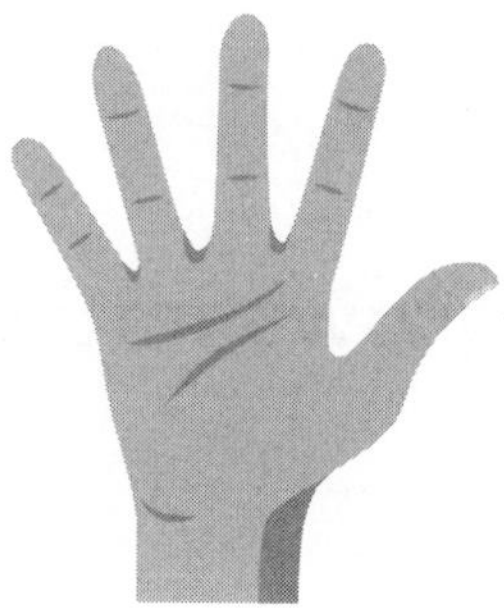

2. Which body part helps you hear?

a. ear

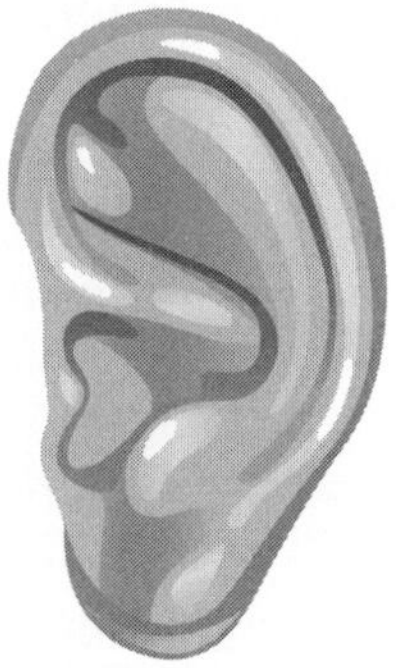

b. nose

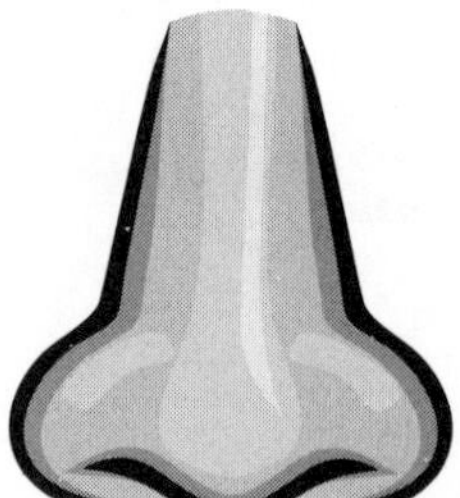

Name: ______________________ Date: ____________

Directions: Look at the chart. Answer the questions.

Five Senses	
see	
hear	
smell	
touch	
taste	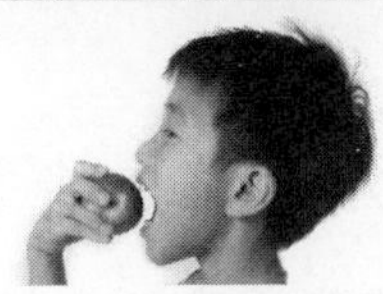

1. What do people use to see?

   a. eyes

   b. headphones

2. I use my sense of touch to ______________.

   a. feel

   b. smell flowers

Name: ____________________ Date: __________

Directions: Read the text. Answer the questions.

Joe comes home from school. His mom baked cookies. Joe asks his mom if he can have one.

1. How does Joe know his mom baked cookies?

a. He saw them.

b. He heard them.

2. Joe wonders if the cookies are ready to eat. Say a question he could ask.

Name: ______________________ **Date:** ____________

Directions: Read the text. Answer the questions.

Ellie plays soccer. She is a goalie. She uses her body to play soccer.

1. What does Ellie use to watch where the ball goes?

a. eyes

b. hands

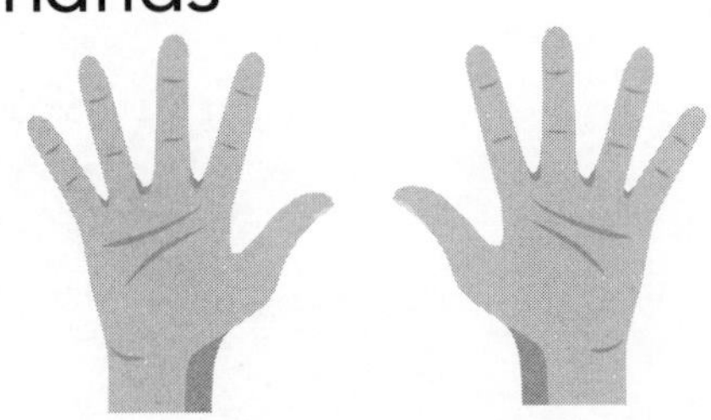

2. What could Ellie do to get the ball to her friend?

a. She can kick the ball with her foot.

b. She can kick the ball with her nose

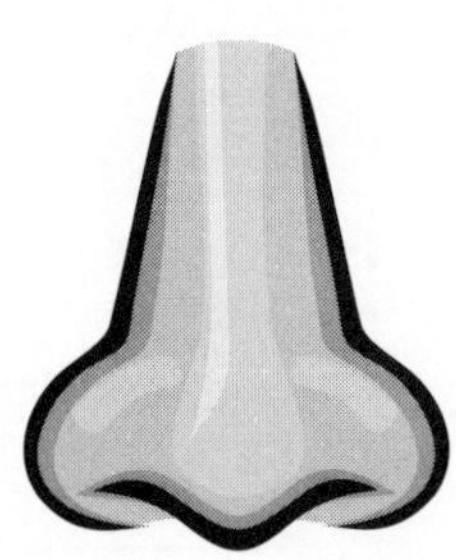

Name: ______________________ **Date:** __________

Directions: Label the parts of the body using the list.

ears	nose	eyes

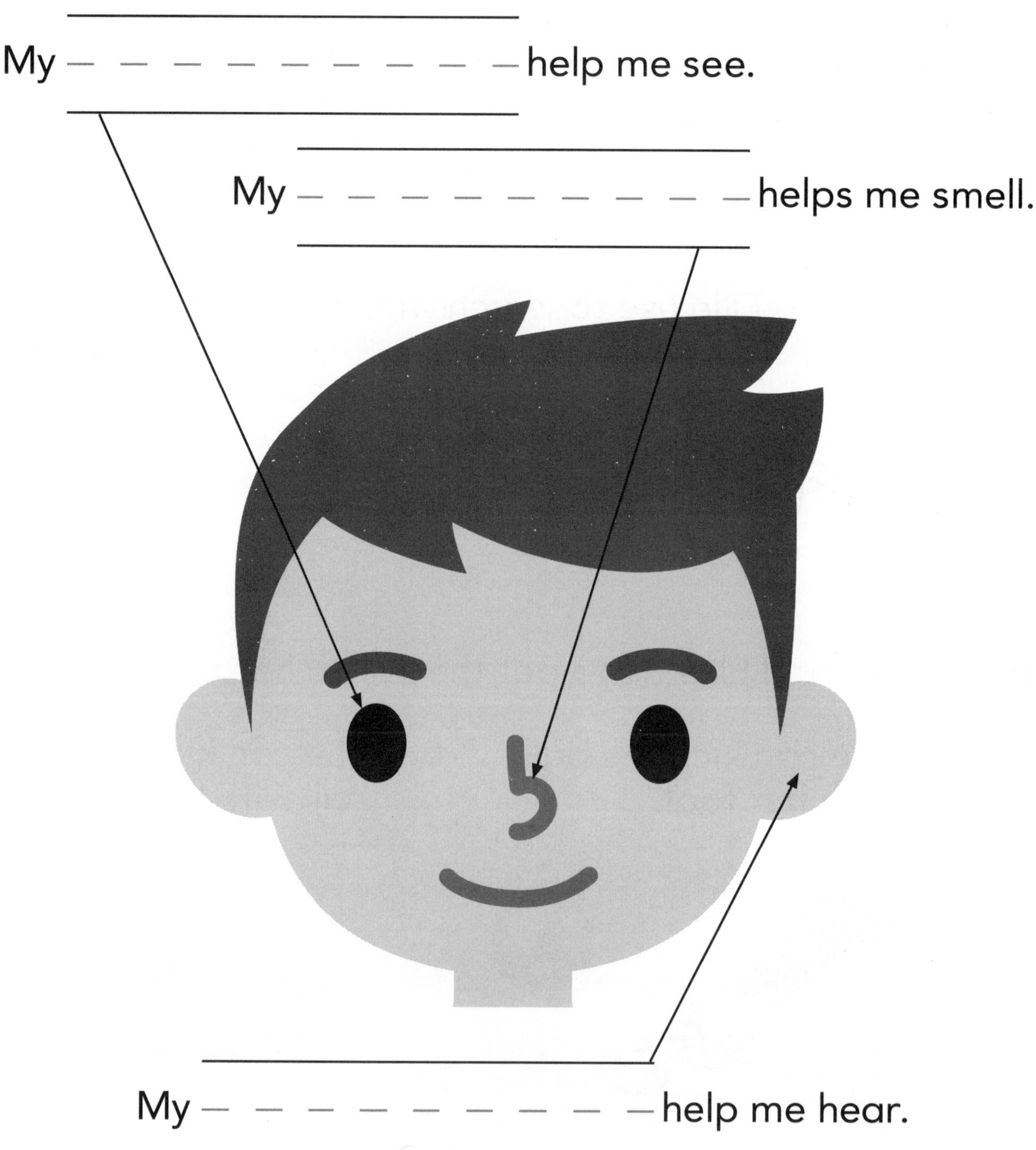

Name: ______________________ **Date:** ____________

Directions: Read the text. Answer the questions.

Animal Bodies

All animals have body parts they need. Fish have fins to swim. Birds have wings to fly. Some animals have strong legs to run fast.

1. Which part of a bird helps it fly?

a. wing 

b. eye 

2. What part of an animal helps it hear?

a. ears 

b. legs 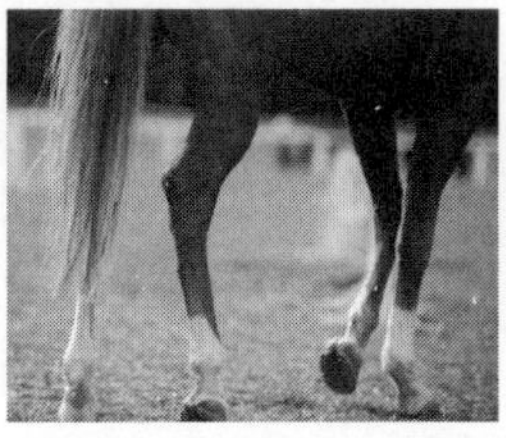

Name: ______________________ **Date:** ____________

Directions: Use the chart to answer the questions.

Body Coverings		
Fur	Feathers	Scales

1. Which animal has fur?

a. rabbit

b. snake

2. How can you tell if an animal is a bird?

a. It has scales.

b. It has feathers.

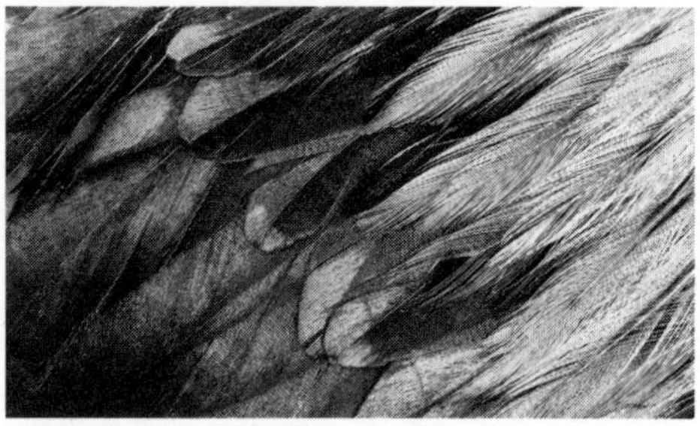

Name: ______________________ **Date:** __________

Directions: Read the text. Answer the questions.

Harry goes to the zoo. He sees a zebra.

1. How does Harry know a zebra can run fast?

   a. It has strong legs. b. It has stripes.

2. Tell a friend a question you have about zebras.

3. Trace the picture below. Then color the picture.

Name: ______________________________ **Date:** ____________

Directions: Think about how you would invent an animal that can fly and walk. Answer the questions.

1. What body part must your animal have to walk?

a. beak

b. legs

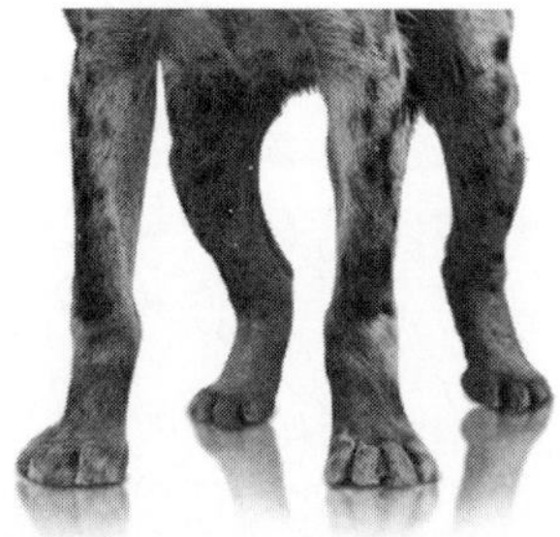

2. How can you test to see if your animal can fly?

a. make it flap its wings

b. give it bird food

Name: ____________________ **Date:** __________

Directions: Draw lines to label the animals' body parts.

1.

eye | tail

mouth | fin

2.

tail | eye

beak | wing

3.

tail | head

leg | eye

Name: ______________________ **Date:** ____________

Directions: Read the text. Answer the questions.

Plant Parts

Plants have many parts. Leaves are above ground. Roots are underground. Roots get water for the plant. Leaves collect sunlight.

1. Roots help plants ____________.

   a. get water

   b. get sunlight

2. Which part of the plant collects sunlight?

   a. leaf

   b. stem

   c. roots

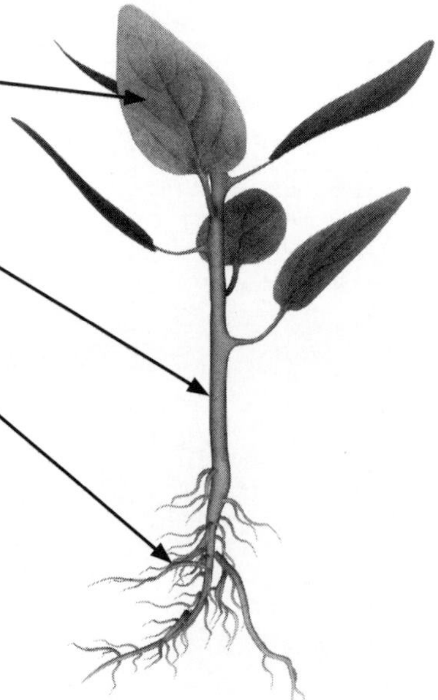

Name: ______________________ **Date:** ____________

Directions: Look at the picture. Answer the questions.

1. Where are the roots of the plant?

   a. above the ground

   b. under the ground

2. Plants do **NOT** have ____________.

   a. mouths

   b. leaves

Name: ______________________________ **Date:** _____________

Directions: Read the text. Answer the questions.

Sofi buys some flowers. She puts the flowers in a vase. She gives them water and sunlight.

1. What part of the flowers does Sofi put in the vase?

a. the leaves

b. the stems

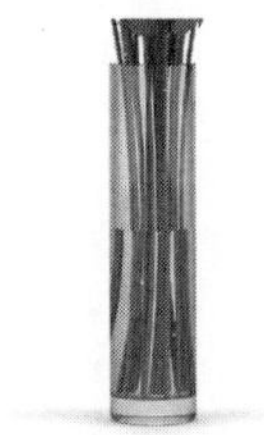

2. Say a question you have about taking care of flowers.

Name: ______________________ **Date:** ____________

Directions: Read the text. Answer the questions.

Elijah sees a plant. It is on the sidewalk. He sees the roots. Roots need to be underground for a plant to grow.

1. What would happen if Elijah left the plant on the sidewalk?

   a. It would stop growing.

   b. It would grow bigger.

2. What could Elijah do to help the plant grow bigger?

   a. Put it back in the ground.

   b. Cut off its roots.

Name: ______________________ Date: __________

Directions: Label the parts of the plant. Then, use the text in the box to help you color the plant.

Color the **flower** red.

Color the **leaves** green.

Color the **stem** yellow.

Color the **roots** brown.

Name: ______________________ Date: ____________

Directions: Read the text. Answer the questions.

Flowers

A flower is part of a plant. The colorful parts are the petals. The stem brings water to the petals. Petals need water to grow and be pretty.

1. What are the colorful parts of a flower called?

a. stem

b. petals

2. What does the stem bring to the flower?

a. light

b. water

Name: ______________________ **Date:** ____________

Analyzing Data

Directions: Look at the chart. Answer the questions.

There are many types of flowers. Some flowers smell good. Some flowers smell bad. Some flowers have seeds you can eat.

	Sunflower 	**Rose** 	**Corpse Lily** 
smells good		**X**	
smells bad			**X**
gives seeds	**X**		

1. Which flower smells good?

a. rose

b. corpse lily

2. Which flower gives seeds you can eat?

a. sunflower **b.** rose

Name: ______________________ **Date:** __________

Directions: Different flowers have different numbers of petals. Look at the chart. Answer the questions.

Flower	lily	iris	buttercup
Petals			

1. Which flower has three petals?

a. lily

b. buttercup

2. How many petals does a buttercup have?

a. three **b.** five

3. Which two flowers have the same number of petals?

a. lily and buttercup **b.** lily and iris

Name: ______________________________ **Date:** ____________

Directions: Read the text. Answer the questions.

Monique buys a pot of flowers. She knows flowers need water to grow.

1. What should Monique do with her flowers?

a. Water them.

b. Put them in the refrigerator.

2. If her flowers start to die, what could Monique do to make them grow?

a. Give them sun and water.

b. Leave them alone.

3. Draw what the flowers need to grow.

Name: ______________________________ **Date:** ____________

Directions: Flowers can look very different, but they are all still flowers. Look at the pictures. Answer the questions.

1. Circle the flowers of each plant.

2. Tell a friend which flower looks most different from the others.

3. Tell a friend which flower is your favorite.

Name: ______________________ Date: ____________

Directions: Read the text. Answer the questions.

Bees and Other Bugs

Not all bugs are the same. Bugs with six legs are called *insects*. Bugs with eight legs are called *arachnids*. A bee has six legs. A spider has eight legs.

1. Why is a bee called an insect?

a. Because it has eight legs.

b. Because it has six legs.

2. Which one is an arachnid?

a. spider

b. fly

Name: ______________________ **Date:** __________

Directions: Look at the picture. Answer the questions.

1. Which body part do you and an insect both have?

a. six legs

b. head

2. Which body part do insects use to fly?

a. wings

b. abdomen

Name: ____________________ Date: __________

Directions: Read the text. Answer the questions.

Bees like colorful flowers. They drink nectar from the flowers. Bees like blue flowers. Bees like purple flowers the best.

1. What can you say about bees?

a. They don't like flowers.

b. They visit flowers.

2. What do bees like best?

a. green leaves

b. purple flowers

3. Say a question you have about nectar.

Name: ______________________ **Date:** ____________

Directions: Read the text. Look at the picture. Answer the questions.

Martin sees a bug. He wants to know what it is. The bug could be an insect. Or the bug could be an arachnid.

1. Which part of the bug should Martin look at first?

   a. the wings

   b. the legs

2. If the bug is an insect, how many legs will it have?

   a. six

   b. eight

3. What test would tell Martin the bug is an insect or an arachnid?

   a. He could count the number of legs.

   b. He could count the number of wings.

Name: ______________________ **Date:** __________

Directions: Insects have six legs. Arachnids have eight legs. Draw the correct number of legs on each bug.

Insect

Arachnid

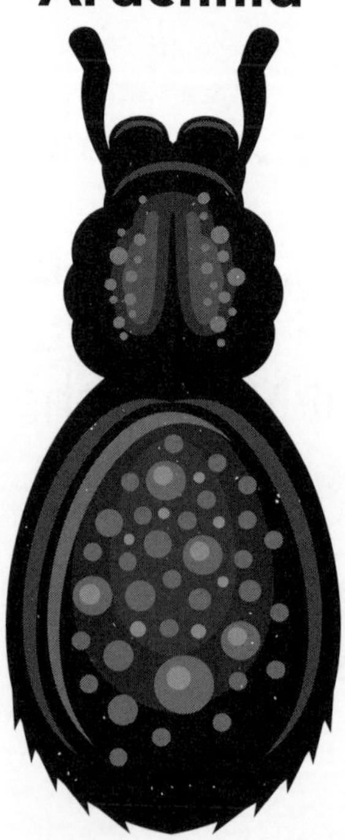

Name: ______________________ **Date:** __________

Directions: Read the text. Answer the questions.

Animal Habitats

Animals need a home. A home is where animals live. A home is where animals raise babies. Animals need a big area to find food and water. This is called a *habitat*.

1. What is something every living thing needs?

a. a car

b. a home

2. What do animals get from their habitats?

a. food and water

b. television

Name: ______________________________ **Date:** ____________

Directions: A home is where an animal lives. A habitat is a large area. A habitat is larger than a home. A habitat is where animals get what they need to live.

1. What is the bird's home?

   a. the whole forest

   b. the nest in the tree

2. What is the bird's habitat?

   a. the whole forest

   b. one tree

Name: ______________________ **Date:** ____________

Directions: Read the text. Answer the questions.

Olivia has a pet hamster. It needs a place to sleep. It needs food and water to live. After food and water, it needs exercise.

1. What is the first thing Olivia should get for her hamster?

   a. food and water

   b. an exercise wheel

2. Say a question Olivia could ask about her hamster's food.

Name: ______________________ **Date:** ____________

Directions: Read the text. Answer the questions.

Ducks live near water. Water is their habitat. These ducks live near a pond. One summer, the pond dries up.

1. What should the mother duck do?

   a. stay and hope the pond fills up

   b. find a new home near some water

2. What else does a duck need in its habitat? Draw a picture of it.

Name: ______________________________ Date: ____________

Directions: Different animals live in different habitats. Match the animal to its habitat.

earthworm

desert

camel

forest

dolphin

underground

deer

ocean

Communicating Results

Name: ______________________ Date: __________

Directions: Read the text. Answer the questions.

Learning Content

Homes and Habitats

Your home sits in a big area. The big area is a habitat. A habitat is where you buy food. A habitat is where you go to school. Many different families can live in the same habitat.

1. How many people can live in a habitat?

   a. one family

   b. many families

2. What is the difference between a home and a habitat?

   a. A habitat is bigger than a home.

   b. A habitat is smaller than a home.

Name: ______________________ **Date:** ____________

Directions: Read the text. Look at the picture. Answer the questions.

A home is where you live. A home is on a street. A street is in a city. A city is a big habitat.

1. Which is bigger, a home or a habitat?

   a. a habitat **b.** a home

2. What is the habitat of this street?

   a. a home **b.** the city

Name: ______________________________ **Date:** ____________

Directions: Read the text. Look at the map. Answer the questions.

Jaime lives in a town. His town has many places to go. His town has many things to do. The town is his habitat.

Developing Questions

1. What is something you see in Jaime's habitat?

   a. a school **b.** a ski slope

2. Say a question Jaime could have about his habitat.

Name: ______________________ **Date:** ____________

Directions: Read the text. Answer the questions.

Your family is moving. Think about what you need in your new home.

1. What do you need in your home?

   a. 

   b. 

2. Which animal makes a park its habitat?

   a. 

   b. 

3. What do you and an animal both need in your habitats?

   a. a place to eat

   b. a place to do homework

Name: ______________________ Date: __________

Directions: Draw a picture of your home in your habitat. Include the things in the box.

school	grocery store
playground	hospital

Name: ______________________ **Date:** __________

Directions: Read the text. Answer the questions.

Baby Animals

Babies don't always look like their parents. Babies are smaller than their parents. Babies can be a different color. But babies are the same animal.

1. Baby animals ______________ .

a. don't look exactly like their parents

b. get food for their parents

2. Which sheep is the baby?

a.

b.

3. Sometimes baby animals are ______________ .

a. a different kind of animal than their parents

b. a different color than their parents

Name: ______________________ **Date:** __________

Directions: Baby animals have different names than adult animals. Look at the pictures. Answer the questions.

Analyzing Data

1. What is a baby cat called?

a. kitten **b.** puppy

2. What is a baby pig called?

a. chick **b.** piglet

3. What is a puppy?

a. a baby dog **b.** a baby chicken

Name: ______________________ **Date:** __________

Directions: Some animals take care of their babies just like adults take care of children. Answer the questions.

1. What do adults do for you?

a. take you to school

b. sleep for you

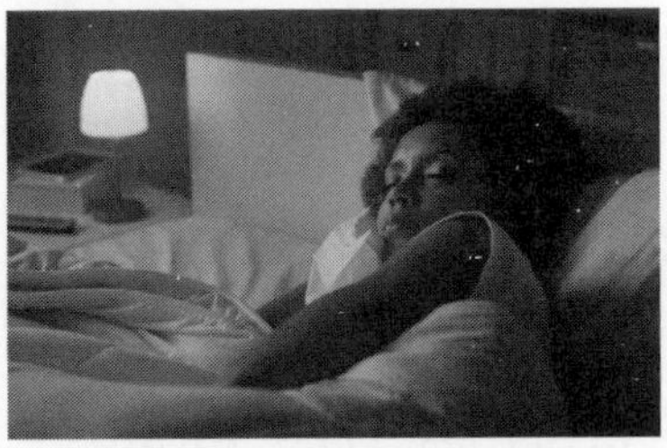

2. What does an animal parent do for its babies?

a. read them a story

b. feed them

3. Say a question you have about kittens.

Name: ______________________ **Date:** ____________

Directions: Look at the picture. Answer the questions.

1. What kind of animals are these?

   a. a lion and a cub **b.** a whale and a pup

2. How is the baby animal different from its parent?

   a. It has more hair. **b.** It has less hair.

3. Draw a baby animal and its parent.

Name: ______________________ **Date:** ____________

Directions: Match the animal with its baby.

frog

joey

dog

chick

kangaroo

tadpole

chicken

puppy

Name: ______________________ **Date:** ____________

Directions: Read the text. Answer the questions.

Seeds to Sprouts

A seed is planted in the ground. The seed grows roots. Then the plant comes out of the ground. It is called a *sprout*. A sprout grows to be an adult plant.

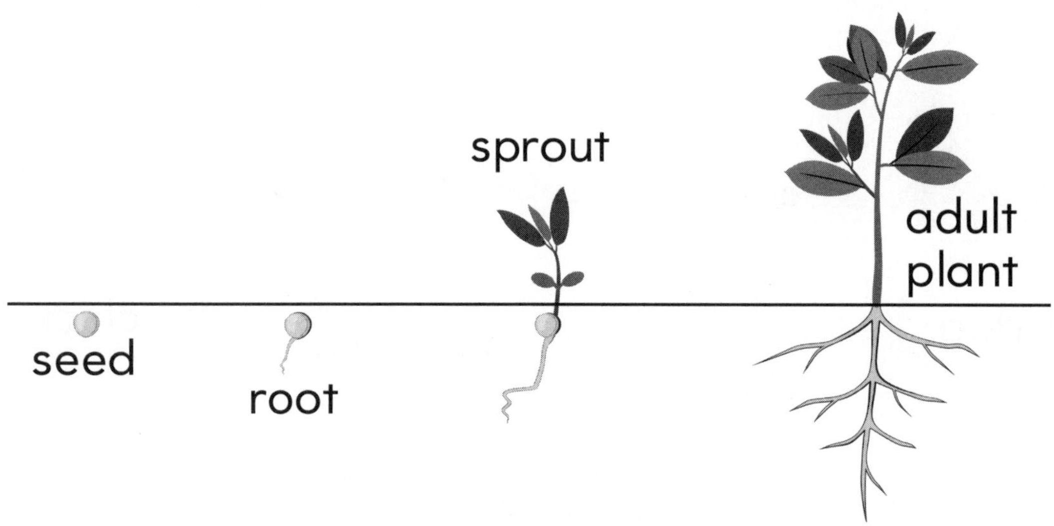

1. How do plants start?

a. as leaves

b. as seeds

2. What is a plant called when it first comes out of the ground?

a. flower

b. sprout

Name: ______________________ **Date:** ____________

Directions: Look at the picture. Answer the questions.

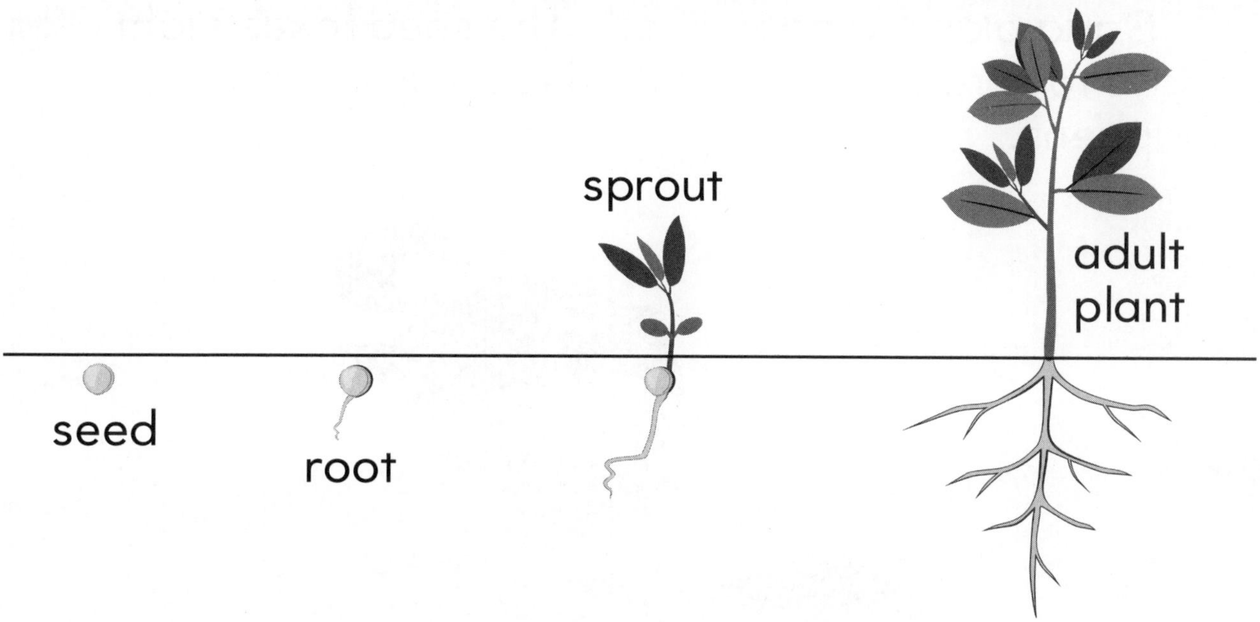

1. What happens first?

a. A seed is planted.

b. The plant grows above ground.

2. How can you tell when a seed becomes a sprout?

a. When it grows roots.

b. When it comes out of the ground.

3. Which way do roots grow?

a. up

b. down

Name: ______________________ **Date:** __________

Directions: Read the text. Answer the questions.

Darla plants a bean seed. The seed takes eight days to sprout. Darla waits three days. Nothing happens.

1. What is happening with Darla's bean seed?

   a. It is growing under the dirt.

   b. It stopped growing.

2. Say a question Darla could ask about her bean seed.

3. Say a question Darla could ask about the dirt.

Name: ______________________ **Date:** ____________

Directions: Read the text. Look at the picture. Answer the questions.

There are two pots with seeds. One pot is near a sunny window. The other pot is in the shade. The pot in the sun grows a sprout in 8 days. The pot in the shade grows a sprout in 10 days.

1. Why did the seed near the window grow faster?

    a. It had a large pot.

    b. It was in the sun.

2. Where will beans sprout faster?

    a. Near a sunny window.

    b. In the closet.

Name: ______________________ **Date:** ____________

Directions: Color the pictures.

Color the seed brown.

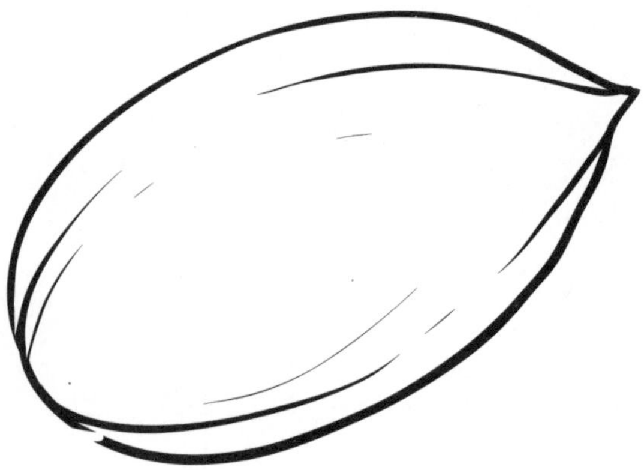

Color the roots yellow.

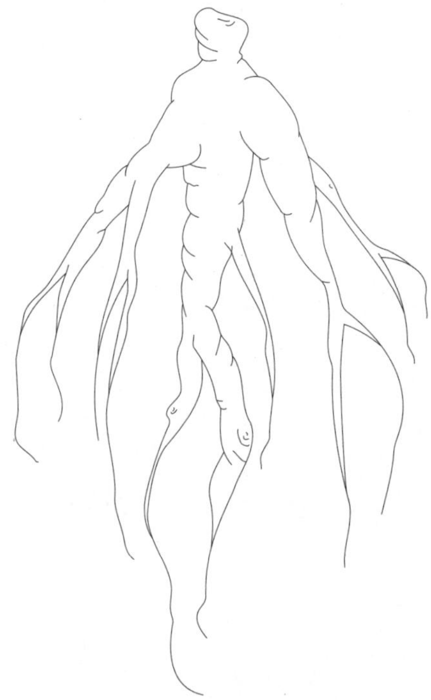

Color the sprout light green.

Color the plant green.

Name: ______________________________ **Date:** ____________

Directions: Read the text. Answer the questions.

Healthy Living

A habit is something you do every day. Habits can be good for you. Good habits keep you healthy. These are good habits.

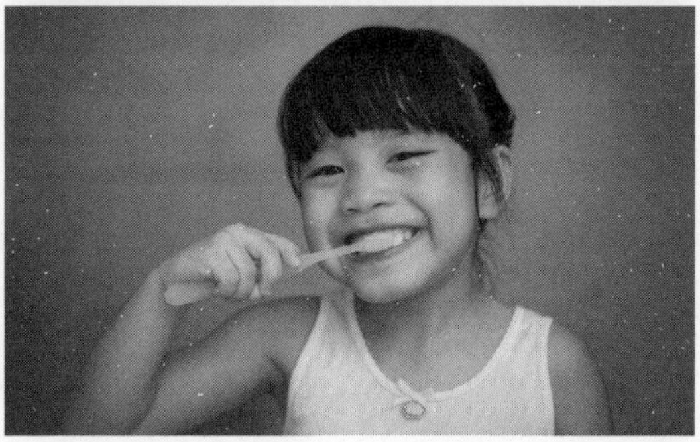

1. What can you do to be healthy?

   a. Stay up late

   b. Brush your teeth

2. What is a habit?

   a. Something you do on your birthday.

   b. Something you do every day.

Name: ______________________ **Date:** __________

Directions: Read the text. Look at the pictures. Answer the questions.

Fruits and vegetables are healthy foods. Cake, doughnuts, and pizza are not healthy foods.

1. Which food is healthy?
   - **a.** cake
   - **b.** carrot
2. Which food is unhealthy?
   - **a.** cake
   - **b.** milk

Analyzing Data

Name: ______________________________ **Date:** ____________

Directions: Answer the questions.

1. Which is a healthy dessert?

   a. candy

   b. fruit

2. What else is a healthy dessert?

   a. yogurt

   b. ice cream

3. Say a question you have about unhealthy food.

4. Say a question you have about healthy food.

Name: ______________________ Date: __________

Directions: Answer the questions.

1. Where can you go to find healthy food?

a. 

b. 

2. How can you eat healthy every day? Draw a picture of what you would eat.

Name: ______________________________ **Date:** ____________

Directions: Read the text. Color the activity that will help you stay healthy.

> It's important to exercise to be healthy. Watching too much TV isn't healthy.

Name: ______________________ **Date:** ____________

Directions: Read the text. Answer the questions.

What Things Are Made Of

Animals are living things. Plants are living things. Things that don't live are called *objects*. Toys and books are objects. Objects can be made of paper, metal, and plastic.

1. Which is the object?

a. fish

b. bike

2. Which is made out of plastic?

a. dog

b. water bottle

Analyzing Data

Name: ______________________________ **Date:** ____________

Directions: Look at the chart. Answer the questions.

Object	Material
	wood
	paper
	glass
	plastic
	metal

1. Which material is a comic book made of?

a. glass

b. paper

2. Which material is the picnic bench made of?

a. wood

b. metal

Name: ______________________ **Date:** ____________

Directions: Read the text. Answer the questions.

Ali got two metal toy trucks for his birthday.

1. How are the two trucks the same?

   a. They are made of metal.

   b. They are the same size.

2. How are the two trucks different?

   a. They are different shapes.

   b. They are different sizes.

3. Say a question Ali could ask about the size of the trucks.

Name: ______________________________ **Date:** ____________

Directions: Read the text. Answer the questions.

You like sports. You have a wooden baseball bat. You have a metal golf club. You have a plastic hula hoop. You keep them under your bed. It is dark under your bed.

1. What can you tell your friend about a baseball bat?

   a. It is made out of wood.

   b. It is made out of plastic.

2. You want the golf club under your bed. You can't see it. How do you know you've grabbed it?

   a. You can feel for a metal object.

   b. You can feel for a wooden object.

Name: ______________________ **Date:** ____________

Directions: Look around you. Find objects made of wood, glass, metal, and plastic. Draw them.

Wood	Glass
Metal	**Plastic**

Name: ______________________ **Date:** ____________

Directions: Read the text. Answer the questions.

Light or Heavy?

Weight tells you how heavy something is. Weight tells you how light something is, too. An elephant is heavy. A feather is light.

1. Which one is heavy?

   a. blue whale

   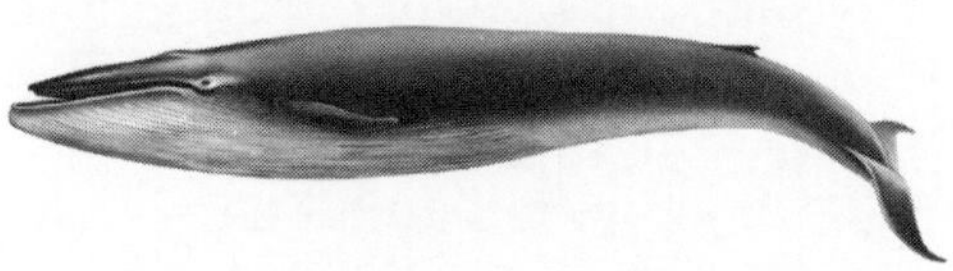

   b. balloon

2. Which one is light?

   a. sofa

   b. strawberry

Name: ______________________ **Date:** ____________

Directions: Read the text. Look at the pictures. Answer the questions.

A scale shows you which object is lighter and which object is heavier.

Lighter or Heavier?

1. Which object is lighter?

   a. bananas

   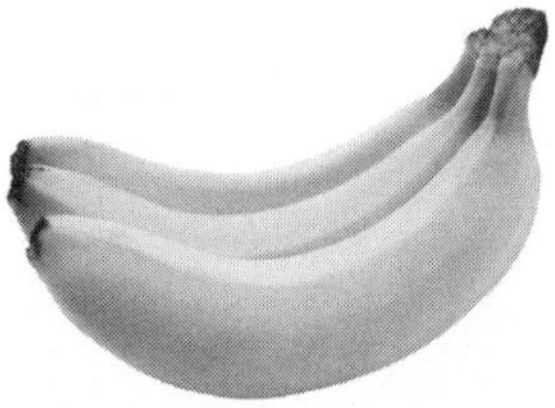

   b. watermelon

2. Is the spoon lighter or heavier than the pan?

   a. lighter

   b. heavier

Name: ____________________ **Date:** __________

Directions: Read the text. Answer the questions.

Shan and his family are moving. Shan wants to help.

1. Which object could Shan lift by himself?

a. skateboard

b. bed

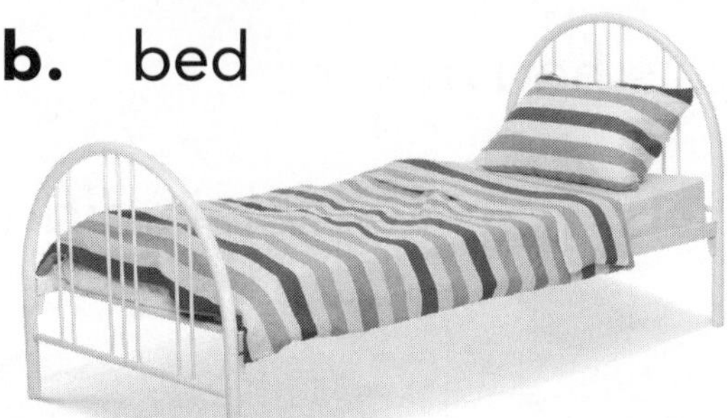

2. Say a question you have about lifting heavy things.

Name: ______________________ **Date:** ____________

Directions: Read the text. Answer the questions.

Your dad needs to bring in grocery bags. He asks you to help.

1. Which grocery bag will be heavy?

a. 

b. 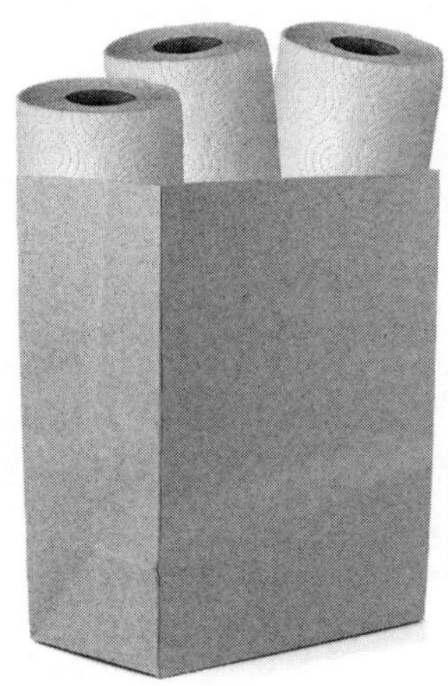

2. How can you test which bag is heaviest?

a. Weigh them.

b. See which is bigger.

Name: ______________________________ Date: ____________

Directions: Look around the room. Find four objects that are light. Find four objects that are heavy. Draw the objects.

Light	Heavy

Name: ______________________ **Date:** ____________

Directions: Read the text. Answer the questions.

How Things Move

Things that move are in motion. Things that are not moving are still. Some objects, like grocery carts, are pushed. Other objects, like a toy wagon, are pulled.

1. Which person is in motion?

a.

b.

2. Which object is being pushed?

a. drawer

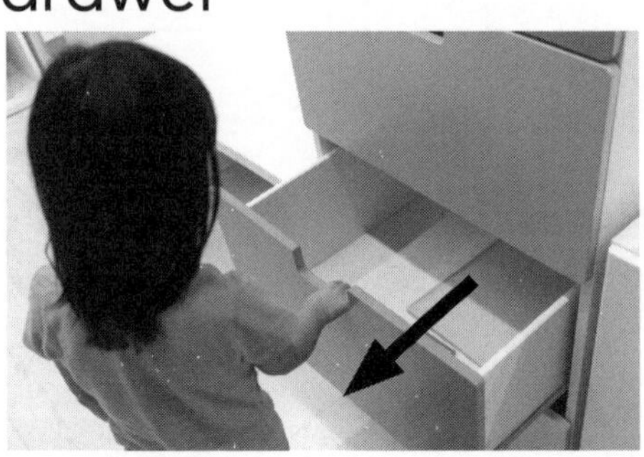

b. door

Name: ______________________________ **Date:** ____________

Directions: Read the text. Look at the pictures. Answer the questions.

When you pull something, you force it towards you. When you push something, you force it away from you.

Push		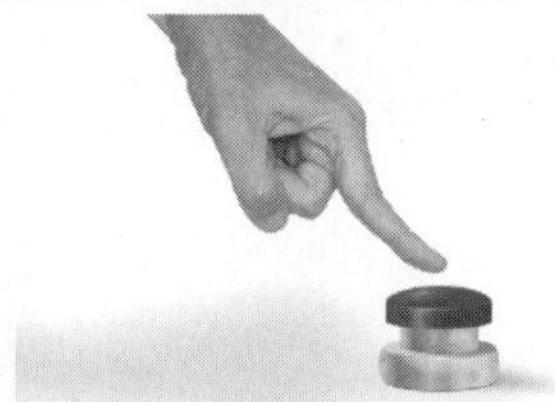	
Pull	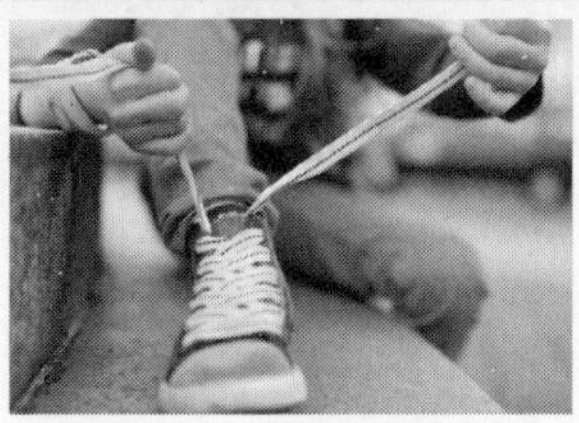		

1. Which object is being pushed?

a. zipper

b. lawnmower

2. Which object is being pulled?

a. shoe laces

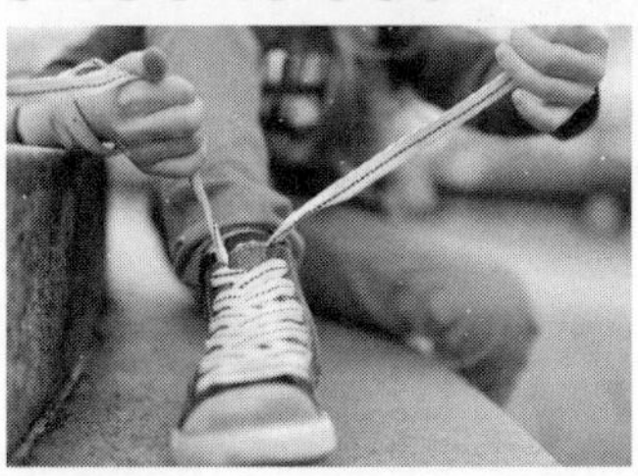

b. button

Name: ______________________ Date: ____________

Directions: Read the text. Answer the questions.

Sang took his dog, Max, for a walk. Max got a pine needle stuck in his paw. It hurt Max. So Sang took Max to the doctor.

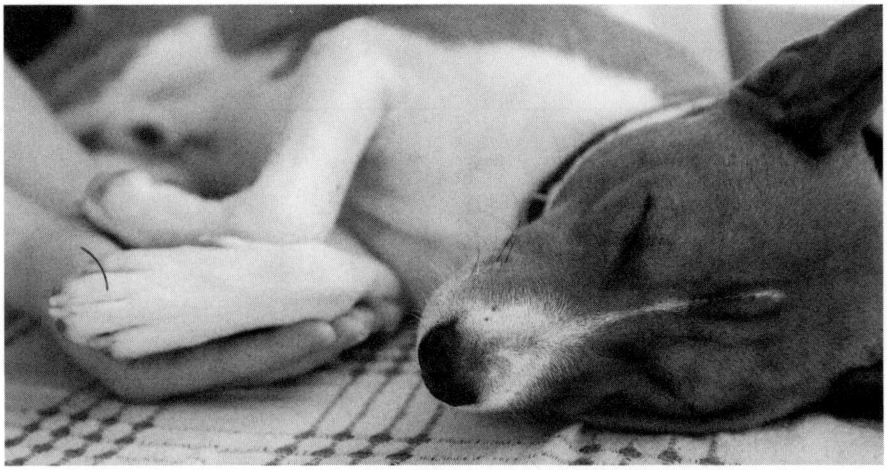

1. What can the doctor do to help Max?

a. Pull the needle out of Max's paw.

b. Push the needle into Max's paw.

2. What was Max doing to get a needle in his paw?

a. He was moving.

b. He was sitting still.

3. Say a question Sang could ask about the needle in Max's paw.

Name: ______________________________ **Date:** ____________

Directions: Read the text. Answer the questions.

Alex got a new a scooter. She wants to show it to her friend. Alex rides the scooter to her friend's house.

1. What can Alex do to make the scooter move?

   a. push the ground with her foot

   b. pull the ground with her foot

2. If Alex stops pushing, the scooter will ____________ .

   a. go faster

   b. slow down

3. What can Alex do to make the scooter stop?

   a.

   b.

Name: ______________________ **Date:** __________

Directions: Look around the room. Draw objects that you push and pull.

Things I Push

Things I Pull

Name: ______________________________ Date: ____________

Directions: Read the text. Answer the questions.

Down to the Ground

Things fall down. Leaves fall down. Rain falls down. Balls fall down when you throw them in the air. When people trip, people fall down.

1. How do things fall?

   a. up b. down

2. What will happen if you throw a ball in the air?

   a. stay in the air b. fall to the ground

Analyzing Data

Name: ______________________ **Date:** ____________

Directions: Look at the pictures below. Answer the questions.

On the ground		
Falling to the ground		

1. Which objects are on the ground?

a. snowflakes

b. cars

2. Which object is falling to the ground?

a. basketball

b. desk

Name: ______________________________ **Date:** ____________

Directions: Read the text. Answer the questions.

It is a windy day. So Benny went to fly his kite. He flew the kite for a long time.

1. What happened to the kite when the wind was blowing?

   a. The kite stayed in the air.

   b. The kite fell to the ground.

2. What happened to the kite when the wind stopped?

   a. It stayed in the air.

   b. It fell to the ground.

3. Say a question Benny could ask about objects that fly.

Name: ______________________ **Date:** ____________

Directions: Read the text. Answer the questions.

Ally likes swimming. Ally likes to jump into her pool. Ally uses her feet to push. She pushes herself up into the air.

1. Where are Ally's feet before she jumps?

a. in the pool

b. on the ground

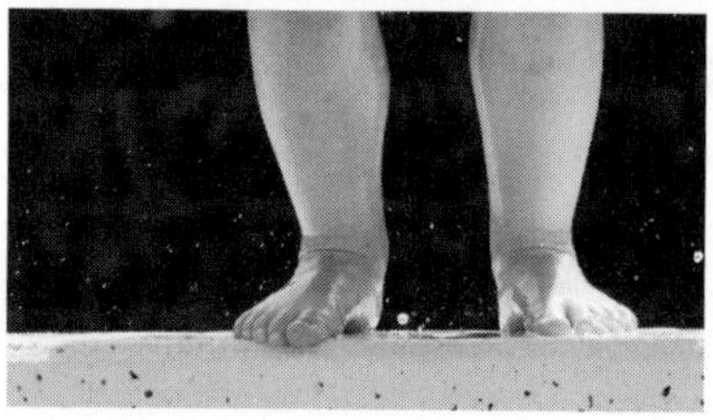

2. What happens after she jumps?

a. She falls down.

b. She floats in the air.

3. What could Ally do to make a big splash?

a. jump higher

b. wear goggles

Name: ______________________________ **Date:** ____________

Directions: Color the things that are in the air. Trace the things that are on the ground.

In the Air	On the Ground

Name: ______________________________ **Date:** ____________

Directions: Read the text. Answer the questions.

Magnets in Motion

Magnets attract. Magnets can pull some objects toward them. Magnets can pull spoons and keys. Magnets can't pull wood or plastic.

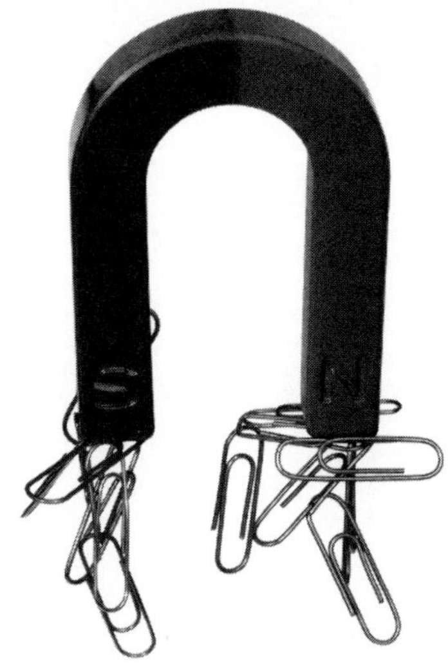

1. What can a magnet do?

   a. Turn objects into a different color

   b. Pull objects toward it

2. What do magnets attract?

   a. pencils

   b. spoons

Name: ______________________________ **Date:** ____________

Directions: Look at the chart. Answer the questions.

Metal 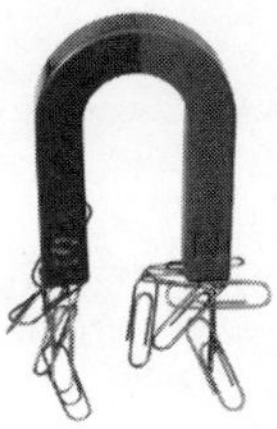	**Not Metal** 

1. Which object could a magnet pull?

a. fork

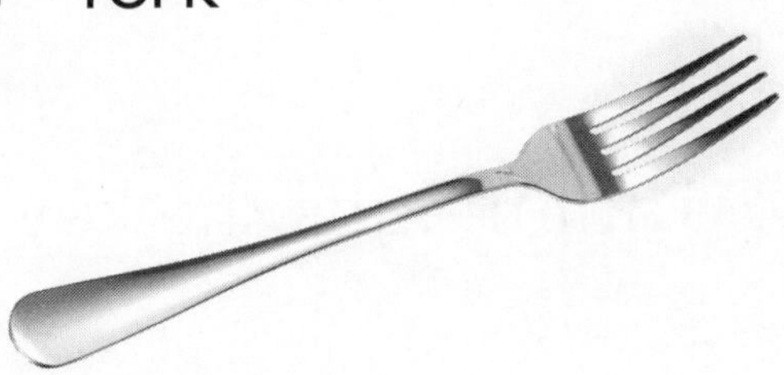

b. apple

2. Which object would be attracted to a magnet?

a. key

b. toothbrush

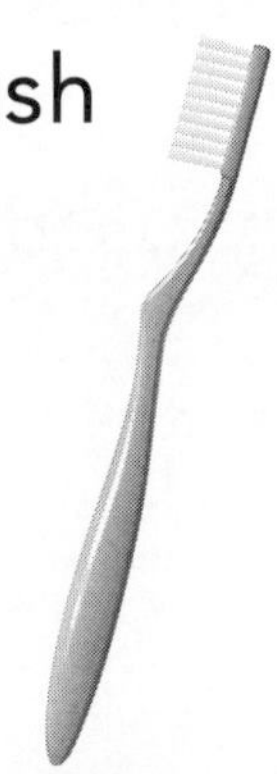

Name: ______________________ **Date:** ____________

Directions: Read the text. Answer the questions.

Sandro has many toys under his bed. There is a metal fire truck under his bed. He wants to get it, but he can't reach it.

1. What will a magnet do to the fire truck?

   a. attract it

   b. push it away

2. The magnet pulls out a key. That means the key is made of ____________ .

   a. wood

   b. metal

3. Say a question Sandro could ask about metals.

Name: ______________________ **Date:** __________

Directions: Read the text. Answer the questions.

Iron is a metal. Iron is everywhere! Iron can be pulled by a magnet. There is iron in sand. Cam plays in a sandbox.

1. Sand contains iron, which is a __________ .

   a. plastic b. metal

2. What can Cam do to pull iron out of the sand?

   a. He can use a magnet. b. He can use a magnifying glass

Communicating Results

Name: ______________________ **Date:** ____________

Directions: Draw a line from the magnetic objects to the magnet.

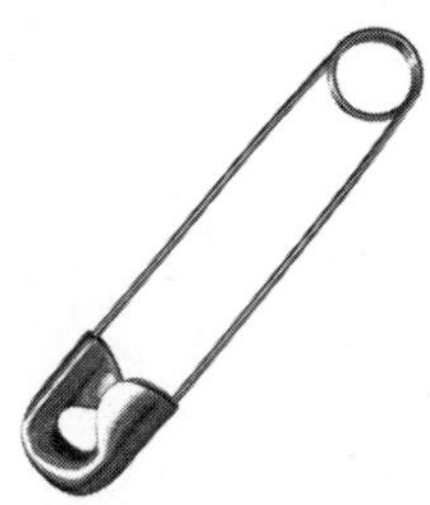

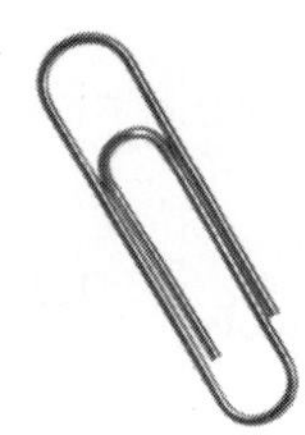

Name: ______________________ Date: ____________

Directions: Read the text. Answer the questions.

Sight

Sight is one of the five senses. Sight lets us see. We see with our eyes. Light helps us see. When it's dark, it's hard to see.

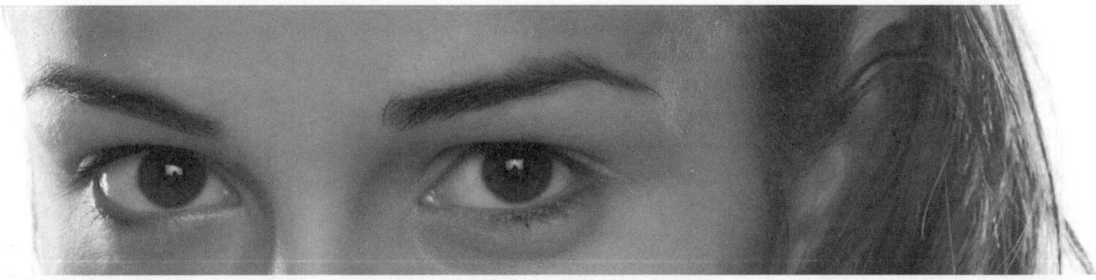

1. Sight is a sense that lets us ____________.

   a. touch **b.** see

2. It's hard to see when it's ____________ outside.

   a. light **b.** dark

Analyzing Data

Name: ______________________ **Date:** __________

Directions: Read the text. Look at the pictures. Answer the questions.

We need light to see. These tools help us see when there is not enough light.

Outside	On the Road	In Your Room

1. Tools help us see when there is not enough ____________.

a. light **b.** time

2. A lamp helps you see in your ____________.

a. room **b.** garden

3. Which tool helps you see when its dark outside?

a. flashlight **b.** headphones

Name: ______________________ **Date:** __________

Directions: Read the text. Answer the questions.

Andi goes bird watching. But the birds are very far away. Andi uses binoculars. Binoculars help Andi see the birds up close.

1. Binoculars help Andi see birds that are ____________.

   a. near

   b. far away

   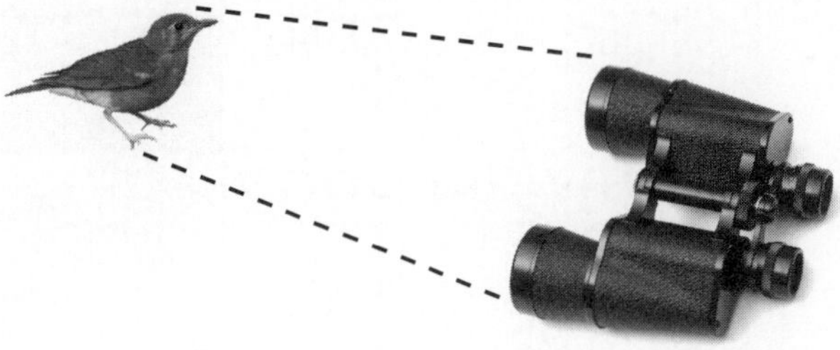

2. How does Andi know there are birds in the park?

   a. She can see them in her binoculars.

   b. Her friend told her.

3. Say a question Andi could have about bird watching at night.

Name: ______________________________ **Date:** ____________

Directions: Read the text. Answer the questions.

It's Halloween. Darryl dresses as a pirate. He wears an eyepatch. He can't see well with an eyepatch. Darryl goes trick or treating. He bumps into a tree.

1. Why can't Darryl see well?

   a. He has an eyepatch.

   b. His candy bag is too heavy.

2. Why did Darryl bump into a tree?

   a. He couldn't see well.

   b. He couldn't hear well.

3. What could Darryl do to see better?

   a. take off his boots

   b. take off his eyepatch

Name: ______________________________ **Date:** ____________

Directions: Draw the eyes on these animals to help them see. Then color the pictures.

lion

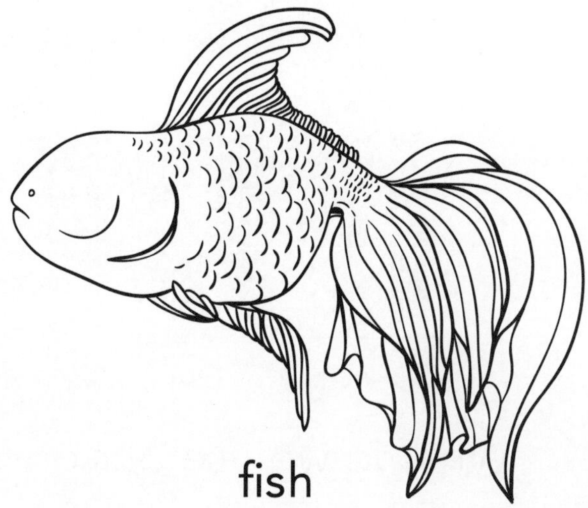

fish

owl

horse

Name: ______________________ **Date:** ____________

Directions: Read the text. Answer the questions.

Sound

Hearing is one of the five senses. We hear with our ears. We hear sounds. Sounds can be loud, like a dog barking. Sounds can be soft, like a whisper.

1. Why do we use our ears?

    a. to hear sounds

    b. to see light

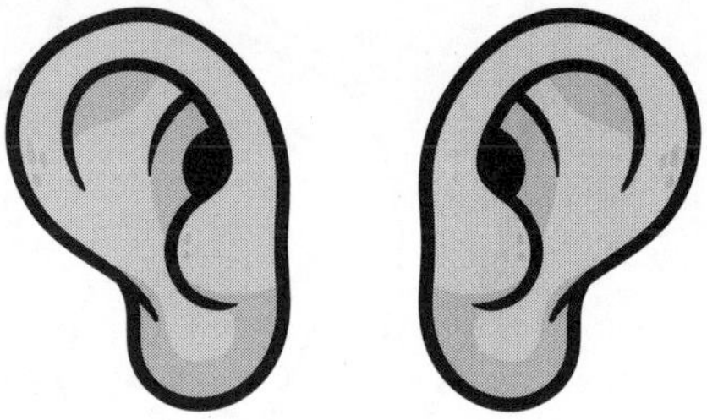

2. Thunder is a ____________ sound.

    a. loud   **b.** soft

3. A whisper is a ____________ sound.

    a. loud

    b. soft

Name: ______________________ Date: ____________

Directions: Look at the chart. Answer the questions.

Loud Sounds	Soft Sounds

1. Which sound is soft?

   a. purring cat

   b. roaring lion

2. Which sound is loud?

   a. banging drums

   b. washing hands

Name: ______________________ **Date:** ____________

Directions: Read the text. Answer the questions.

Developing Questions

Javier hears people screaming. They are on a roller coaster. The sound is soft. When he walks closer, the screaming is loud!

1. What do the screams sound like when Javier is far away?

   a. soft

   b. loud

2. Where are the loud screams coming from?

   a. far away

   b. close

3. Say a question Javier could ask about sounds.

Name: ____________________ **Date:** __________

Directions: Read the text. Answer the questions.

Rosa listens to loud music. She wears headphones. Rosa's mom talks to her. Her mom's lips move. But Rosa can't hear her mom.

1. How does Rosa know her mom is talking?

   a. She can see her lips move.

   b. She can see her eyes blink.

   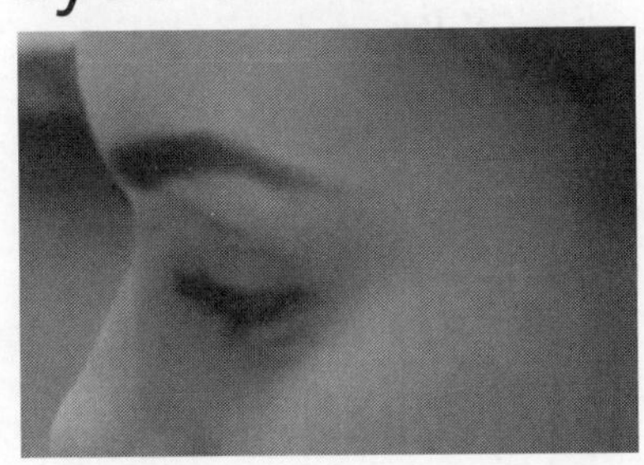

2. What will happen if Rosa takes off her headphones?

   a. She will hear her mom.

   b. She will not not hear her mom.

3. What could Rosa do to hear her mom and her music?

   a. turn down the music

   b. make the music louder

Name: ______________________ **Date:** ____________

Directions: Read the text. Follow the steps.

Which child hears the dogs barking the loudest? Color their clothes red. Who hears the dogs the softest? Color their clothes blue. Color the rest of the picture.

Name: ______________________ Date: __________

Directions: Read the text. Answer the questions.

Smell

We use our noses to smell. We smell through our nostrils. Smells can be good, like baked cookies! Smells can be bad, like rotten fish.

1. What do we use to smell?

a. our nose

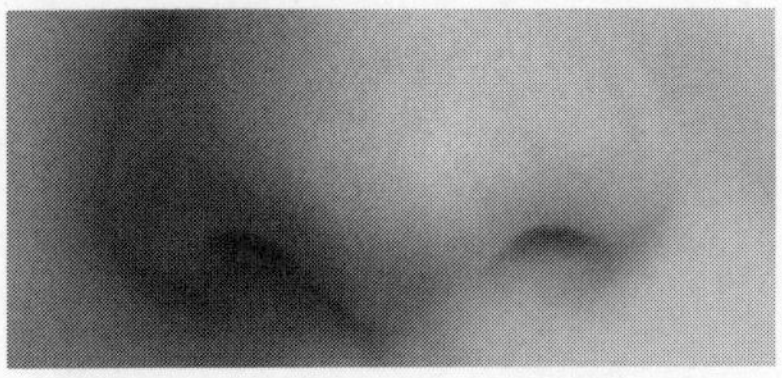

b. our eyes

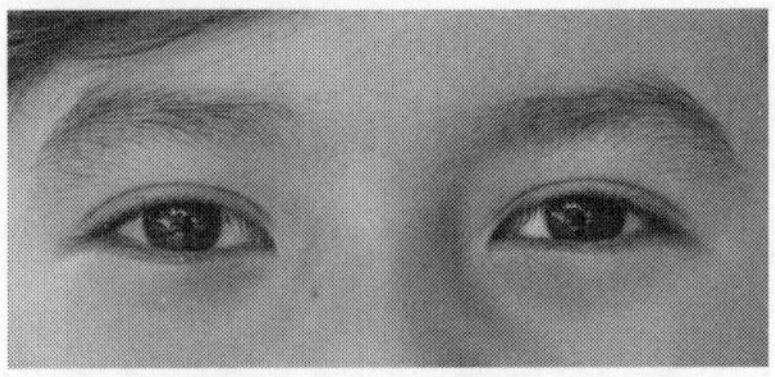

2. Which food smells bad?

a. fresh-baked cookies

b. rotten fish

Analyzing Data

Name: ______________________________ **Date:** ____________

Directions: Look at the chart. Answer the questions.

Good Smells	Bad Smells

1. Which smells good?

a. roses

b. trash

2. Which smells bad?

a. dirty socks

b. apple pie

Name: ______________________ **Date:** ____________

Directions: Read the text. Answer the questions.

Adam is hungry. He opens the fridge. He plugs his nose. Some food went bad. It is rotten.

1. Why did Adam plug his nose?

   a. The food went bad. **b.** His nose was itchy.

2. What would happen if he plugged his nose?

   a. He won't be able to smell. **b.** He won't be able to see.

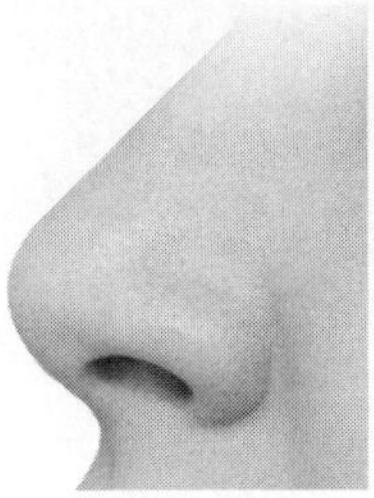

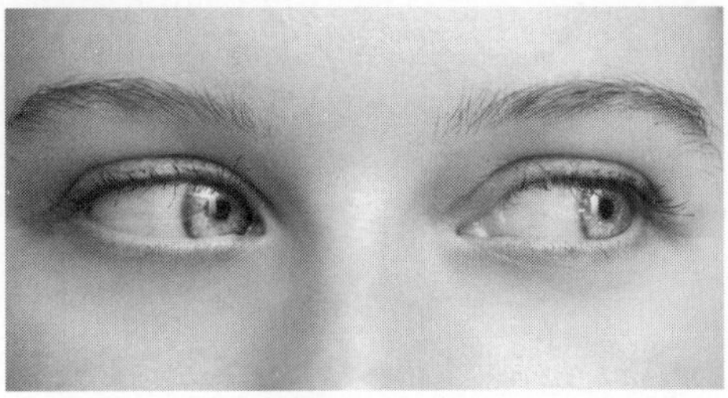

3. Say a question Adam could ask about smells.

Name: ______________________ **Date:** __________

Directions: Read the text. Answer the questions.

Alana likes to smell flowers. She likes roses. When she smells red roses, she sneezes. When she smells yellow and pink roses, she doesn't sneeze.

1. What happens when she smells red roses?

a. She laughs. **b.** She sneezes.

2. What could Alana do **NOT** to sneeze?

a. smell pink roses

b. smell red roses

3. What else could Alana do not to sneeze?

a. plug her nose

b. close her eyes

Name: ______________________ Date: ____________

Directions: Draw three things you like to smell.

I like to smell...

I like to smell...

I like to smell...

Name: ______________________ **Date:** __________

Directions: Read the text. Answer the questions.

Taste

We taste food with our tongues. Food can taste sweet, like cake. Food can taste salty, like potato chips. Food can also taste sour, like lemons. Food can taste bitter, like Brussels sprouts.

1. What do we use to taste?

   a. tongue **b.** hands

2. Which food tastes sweet?

   a. lemon **b.** cake

Name: ______________________________ **Date:** ______________

Directions: Look at the chart. Answer the questions.

	Bitter	**Sweet**	**Salty**	**Sour**
grapefruit 		X		X
potato chips 			X	
cupcake 		X		
spinach 	X			

1. Which food tastes salty?

a.

b.

2. Grapefruit is both sweet and ______________.

a. salty **b.** sour

Name: ______________________ **Date:** ____________

Directions: Read the text. Answer the questions.

Keisha likes eating sweet foods with salty foods. She wants to try foods that are sweet and salty.

1. What could Keisha eat with salty popcorn?

   a. chocolate

   b. celery

2. What could Keisha do to make her peanut butter sandwich sweet?

   a. add strawberry jelly

   b. add lemon slice

3. Say a question Keisha could have about sweet foods.

Name: ______________________ **Date:** ____________

Directions: Read the text. Answer the questions.

When Jamal eats cake, he smiles. When he drinks lemonade, he shuts his eyes. When he eats spinach, he sticks out his tongue.

1. If Jamal makes this face, what did he have?

   a. lemonade

   b. candy bar

2. What could Jamal do to make lemonade sweeter?

   a. He could add salt to it.

   b. He could add sugar to it.

Name: ______________________ Date: ____________

Directions: Draw your favorite foods for breakfast, lunch, and dinner.

Breakfast

Lunch

Dinner

Name: ______________________ **Date:** ____________

Directions: Read the text. Answer the questions.

Touch

We use our hands to feel. Things can feel soft, like a cat. Things can be hard, like a rock. Things can also feel sticky, like glue. Things can be cold, like ice.

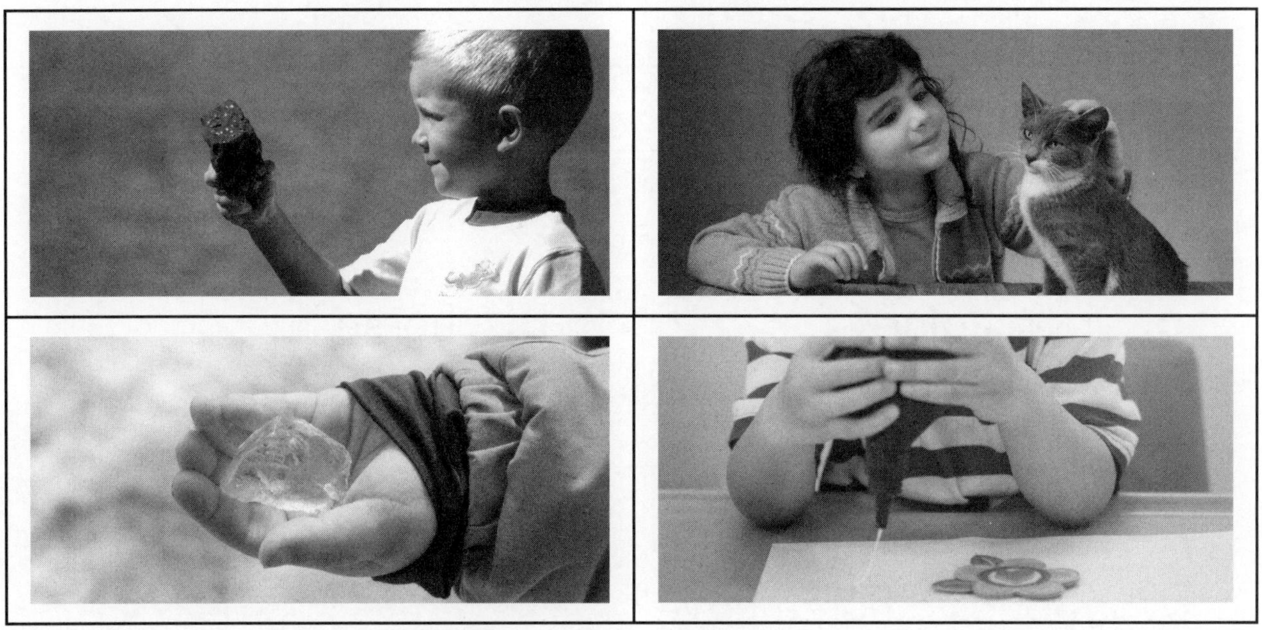

1. Which one is soft?

a. 

b. 

2. Which food is hard?

a. marshmallows

b. lollipops

Name: ______________________ **Date:** __________

Directions: Look at the chart. Answer the questions.

Soft	X	X	
Sharp			X
Smooth		X	

1. Which animal has sharp spines?

   a. porcupine

   b. horse

2. What does a horse have?

   a. smooth hair

   b. sharp hair

Name: ______________________________ **Date:** ____________

Directions: Read the text. Answer the questions.

Aldo likes waffles. He takes waffles out of the fridge. He puts them in a toaster. He likes to put maple syrup on them. Maple syrup is sticky.

1. How do the waffles feel when Aldo takes them out of the fridge?

   a. cold

   b. hot

2. How does the maple syrup feel when Aldo gets it on his fingers?

   a. dry

   b. sticky

3. What happens to the waffle in the toaster?

   a. They warm up.

   b. They stay cold.

Name: ______________________ **Date:** ____________

Directions: Read the text. Answer the questions.

Lars wears a coat outside. It is sunny. Lars feels warm. When he plays, he feels hot. He starts to sweat.

1. How does Lars feel when he goes outside?

a. warm **b.** cold

2. How does Lars feel when he sweats?

a. wet **b.** dry

3. What could Lars do to not feel hot?

a. wear a hat

b. take off his coat

Name: ______________________________ Date: ____________

Directions: Look at the pictures. Draw something you could touch in each place.

Beach

Snow

Classroom

Playground

Name: ______________________ **Date:** ____________

Directions: Read the text. Answer the questions.

Solid, Liquid, Gas

Everything around us is a solid, liquid, or gas. Apples are solids. So is a lunchbox. Milk is a liquid. Clouds are made of gases. So is steam from a hot drink.

solid

liquid

gas

1. Which is a solid?

a.

b.

2. What is steam?

a. a gas

b. a liquid

Name: ______________________ **Date:** ____________

Directions: Look at the chart. Answer the questions.

Solid	**Liquid**	**Gas**
shoes 	water 	smoke 
hamburger 	honey 	air 

1. Which is a solid?

a. sneakers

b. smoke

2. What is honey?

a. a solid

b. a liquid

Name: ______________________ **Date:** ____________

Directions: Read the text. Answer the questions.

Levi has a pond in his yard. In the summer, he swims in the water. In the winter, he skates on the ice.

1. What is Levi's pond in the summer?

   a. a liquid **b.** a solid

2. When does Levi's pond become a solid?

   a. in the winter when it's ice **b.** in the summer when it's water

3. Ask a question Levi could have about liquids and solids.

Name: ______________________________ **Date:** ____________

Directions: Read the text. Answer the questions.

Jenny eats an ice pop. Jenny goes outside in the hot sun. She puts the ice pop down. When she picks it up again, it has melted. It's now a liquid.

1. What is the ice pop after it melted?

a. a liquid **b.** a solid

2. What was the ice pop before it melted?

a. a solid **b.** a gas

3. How can Jenny keep the ice pop solid longer?

a. Eat it in the hot sun.

b. Eat it inside.

Name: ________________________ **Date:** ____________

Directions: Color the solids green and brown. Color the liquids blue. Color the gases yellow.

Name: ______________________________ **Date:** ____________

Directions: Read the text. Answer the questions.

Science Tools

Science tools help us. A ruler helps us measure. A microscope helps us see things up close. A thermometer tells us how hot or cold it is. A clock tells us the time.

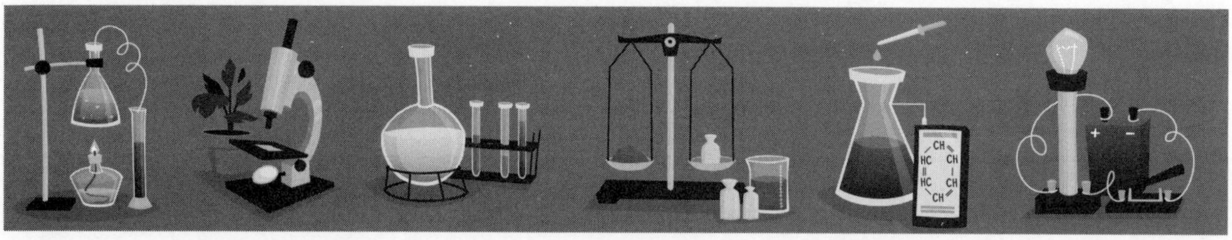

1. What do people use to measure how long a pencil is?

a.

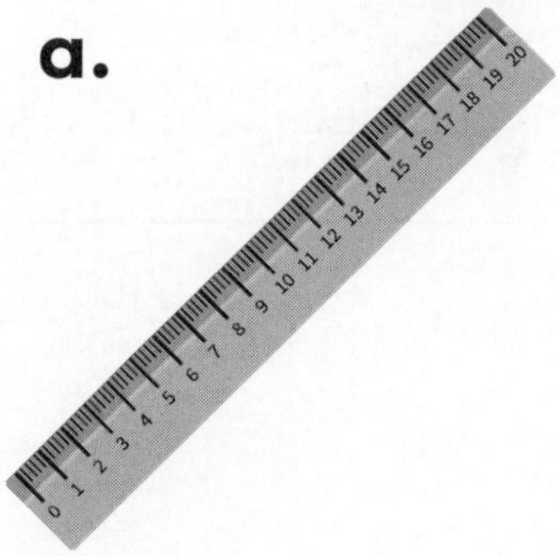

b.

2. What do people use to measure how hot it is?

a. thermometer

b. microscope

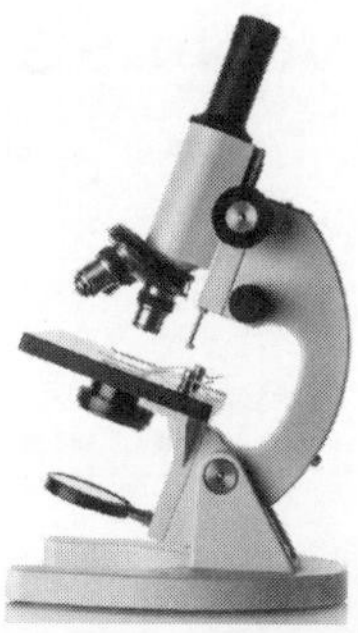

Name: ______________________ **Date:** ____________

Directions: Look at the chart. Answer the questions.

Helps me See	Helps me Measure	Helps me Find
microscope 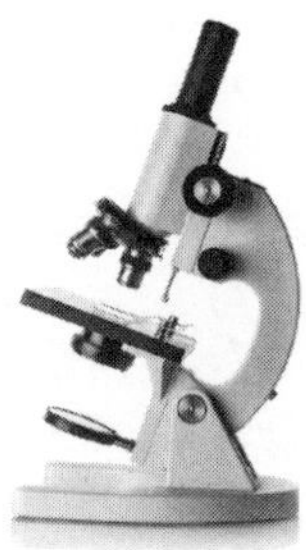	ruler 	globe 
telescope 	measuring cup 	map 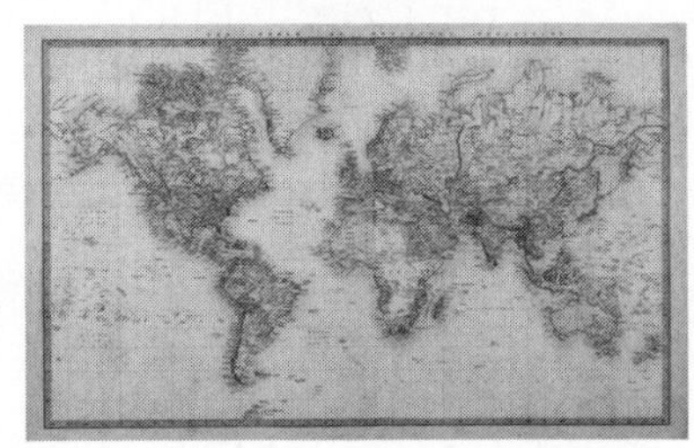

1. What do you use to find a country?

a. 

b. 

2. What do you use to see things far away?

a. 

b. 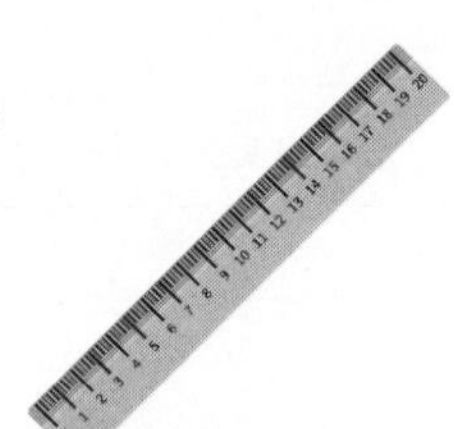

Name: ______________________________ **Date:** ____________

Directions: Read the text. Answer the questions.

Ron has a fever. His head feels warm. His dad uses tools to help him. He also gives Ron medicine.

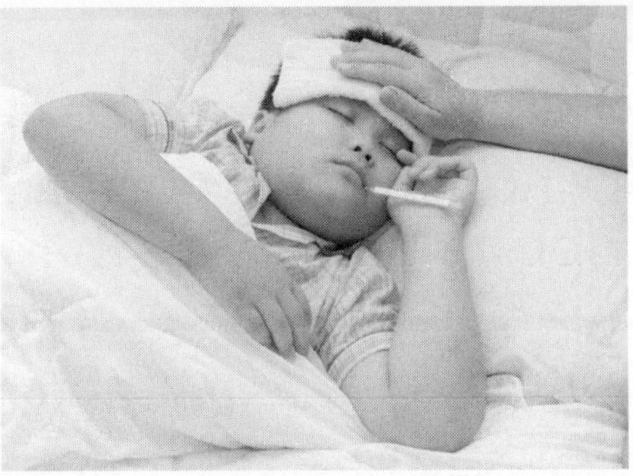

1. What does Ron's dad use to check his temperature?

a. thermometer

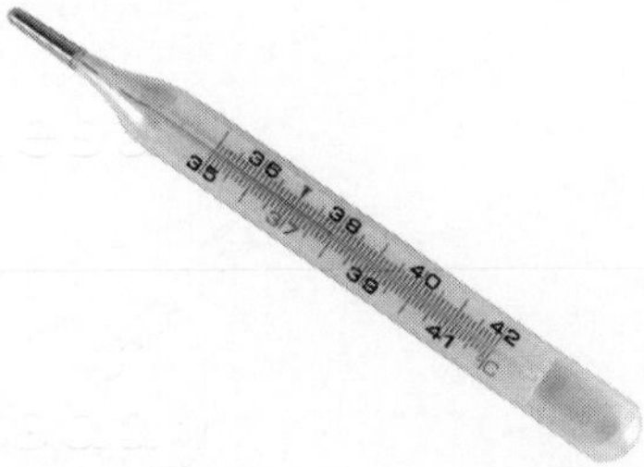

b. scale

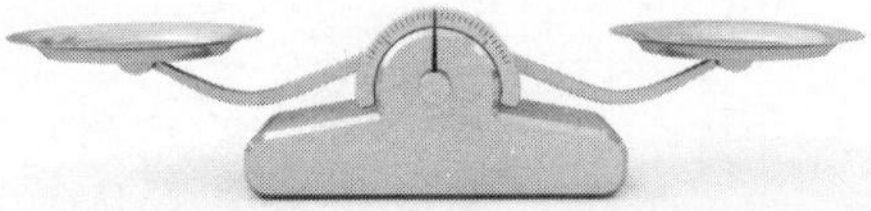

2. What does Ron's dad use to give him the right amount of medicine?

a. measuring cup

b. mug

3. Say a question Ron could ask about tools.

Name: ______________________ **Date:** __________

Directions: Read the text. Answer the questions.

Lana goes to the park. Lana takes a magnifying glass. The magnifying glass lets her see things up close. She takes binoculars to see things far away.

1. What can Lana use to see deer in the park?

a. binoculars

b. magnifying glass

2. Lana wants to know when she saw the deer. What could she do?

a. look at the sky

b. look at her watch

Name: ______________________________ Date: ____________

Directions: Color the toys red. Color the tools blue.

Toy or tool?	

	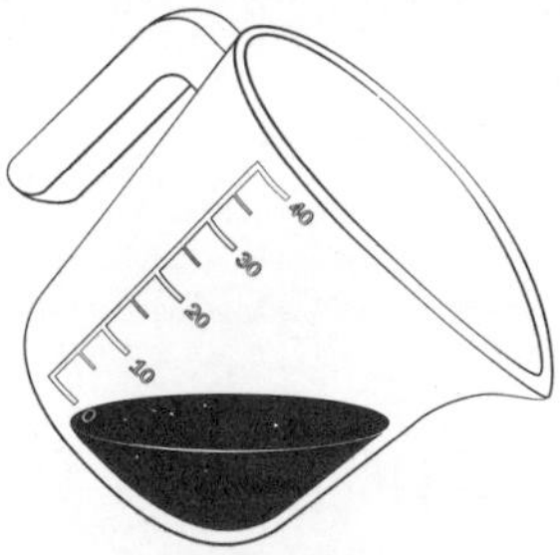

	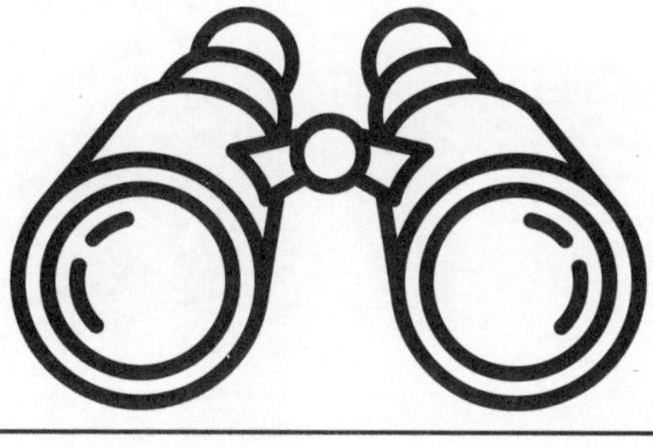

Name: ______________________ **Date:** ____________

Directions: Read the text. Answer the questions.

Weather Patterns

Weather is around us all the time. The weather can be sunny. It can be rainy. It can also be snowy and windy. The weather can be hot or cold.

1. In the summer, the weather is often ____________.

a. sunny

b. snowy

2. In the winter, the weather is often ____________.

a. hot

b. cold

Name: ______________________ Date: ____________

Directions: Look at the chart. Answer the questions.

Weather	Activity
sunny 	
snowy 	
windy 	
rainy 	

1. What is the best weather for flying a kite?

a. windy

b. rainy

2. What can you build when it is snowing?

a. sandcastle

b. snowman

Name: ______________________ **Date:** ____________

Directions: Read the text. Answer the questions.

You can play baseball in the summer. You can go sailing in the summer, too. In the winter, you can play hockey and go skiing.

1. Which sport is often played in the winter?

a. hockey

b. baseball

2. What else can you do in the winter?

a. go skiing

b. go sailing

3. Say a question about playing outside in the winter.

Name: ______________________________ **Date:** ____________

Directions: Read the text. Answer the questions.

It is summer. Jayda looks up in the sky. Jayda sees many gray clouds. Jayda hears thunder. If she sees lightning, she should go inside.

1. What might the weather do next?

a. rain

b. snow

2. If it starts to rain, what should Jayda do?

a. wear a raincoat

b. wear sunglasses

3. What should Jayda do if she sees lightning?

a. go inside

b. wear boots

Name: ______________________ **Date:** ____________

Directions: Draw what you should wear in each type of weather.

Weather	What I Should Wear
hot 	
rainy 	
windy 	
snowy 	

Name: ______________________ **Date:** ____________

Directions: Read the text. Look at the chart. Answer the questions.

Seasonal Changes

There are four seasons. In the winter, it can be cold with snow. In the spring, it can be warm and rainy. The summer can be hot and sunny. In the fall, you might see gray clouds and the leaves may change color.

Winter	Spring	Summer	Fall

1. When is the weather usually hot and sunny?

a. summer **b.** fall

2. What will the ground look like in the winter?

a. snow

b. sand

Analyzing Data

Name: ______________________________ **Date:** ______________

Directions: Study the chart. Answer the questions.

Weather at Clear Lake	
winter 	spring 
summer 	fall 

1. What happens in the spring at Clear Lake?

    a. ice melts   b. lake turns to ice

2. What happens in the winter at Clear Lake?

    a. The lake bubbles.   b. The lake is frozen.

3. Which can you do in the summer in Clear Lake?

    a. go canoeing   b. go ice skating

Name: ______________________ **Date:** ____________

Directions: Read the text. Answer the questions.

Marvin has a tree in his yard. In the winter, the tree has no leaves. In the spring, it rains and leaves grow. Many leaves grow in the summer. In the fall, the leaves change color and fall to the ground.

Winter	Spring	Summer	Fall

1. Leaves on the tree start to grow in the ______________ .

   a. spring

   b. winter

2. Say a question about the tree in warm weather.

3. Say a question about the tree in cold weather.

Name: ______________________________ **Date:** ______________

Directions: Read the text. Answer the questions.

William goes back to school in the fall. The weather is cool. It's windy, too. He needs to wear the right clothes.

1. What should he wear when it's cool and windy?

a.

b.

2. What can William buy to plan for winter?

a.

b.

Name: ______________________ **Date:** ____________

Directions: Match each activity to the right season.

 winter •	•  plant a garden
 spring •	•  picking pumpkins
 summer •	•  skiing
 fall •	•  swimming

Name: ______________________ **Date:** __________

Directions: Read the text. Answer the questions.

Winter Wonders

Winter is the coldest season. Many flowers can't grow. It's too cold. Birds fly to warmer climates. Bears hibernate in the winter. That means they sleep most of the time.

1. Which season is usually the coldest?

a. spring **b.** winter

2. Where do birds fly in the winter?

a. warmer climates **b.** colder climates

3. What do bears do in the winter?

a. sleep **b.** play

Name: ______________________________ **Date:** ____________

Directions: Look at the graph. Answer the questions.

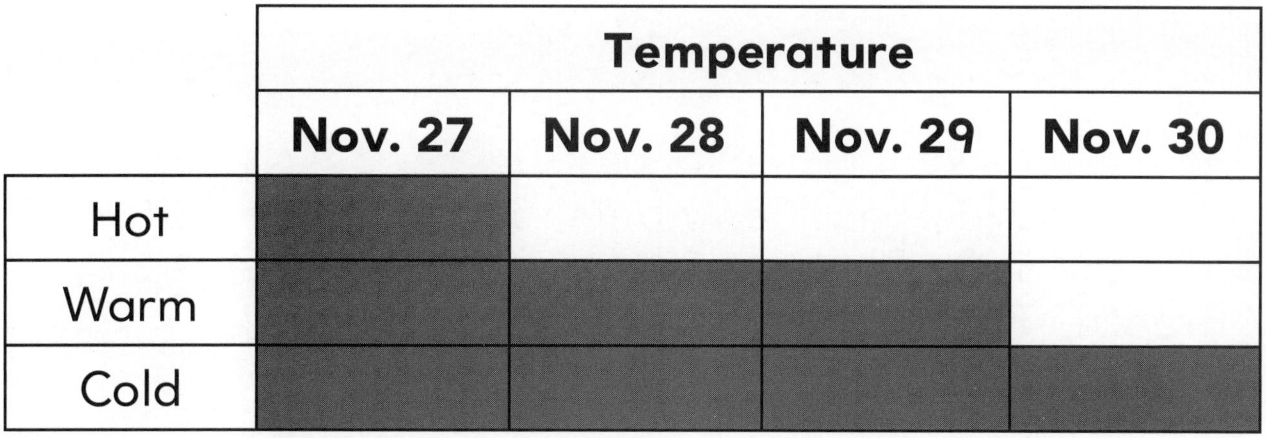

1. Which day was warmest?

   a. Nov. 27

   b. Nov. 30

2. Which day was the coldest?

   a. Nov. 28

   b. Nov. 30

3. What is happening to the temperature?

   a. It is getting colder.

   b. It is getting warmer.

Name: ______________________ **Date:** ____________

Directions: Read the text. Answer the questions.

Jed has a pond. Jed wants to play hockey on it. The pond is starting to freeze. The pond isn't totally frozen. Jed taps the ice with his stick. The ice cracks.

1. Why is the pond starting to freeze?

   a. It is cold outside. **b.** It is warm outside.

2. Why did the ice crack?

   a. It isn't totally frozen. **b.** It isn't a liquid.

3. Say a question Jed could have about his pond.

Name: ______________________ **Date:** ____________

Directions: Read the text. Look at the weather calendar. Answer the questions.

Green Mountain gets lots of rain. Green Mountain gets no snow. White Mountain gets lots of snow. Matt wants to go skiing. He studies the weather calendar.

	Green Mountain 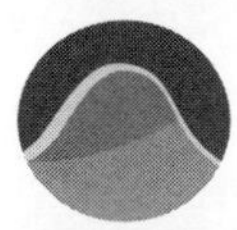	**White Mountain** 
Tuesday		
Wednesday		
Thursday		
Friday		

1. What will probably happen on Friday at White Mountain?

   a. It will rain. **b.** It will snow.

2. Where should Matt plan to ski on Friday?

   a. Green Mountain **b.** White Mountain

Communicating Results

Name: ______________________ **Date:** ____________

Directions: Draw ice skaters, skiers, and a snowman. Then, color the picture.

Name: ______________________________ Date: ____________

Directions: Read the text. Answer the questions.

Spring Things

Spring comes after winter. In the spring, the weather turns warm. It can also rain. In the spring, leaves grow on trees. Flowers also bloom. Flowers attract bees.

1. What comes after winter?

a. spring **b.** summer

2. What happens to the weather in the spring?

a. It turns warm. **b.** It turns cold.

3. What do flowers attract?

a.

b.

Name: ______________________ **Date:** __________

Directions: Read the text. Look at the chart. Answer the questions.

> Bethany keeps a jar outside her window. She uses the jar to see how much rain has fallen.

March	April	May	June
	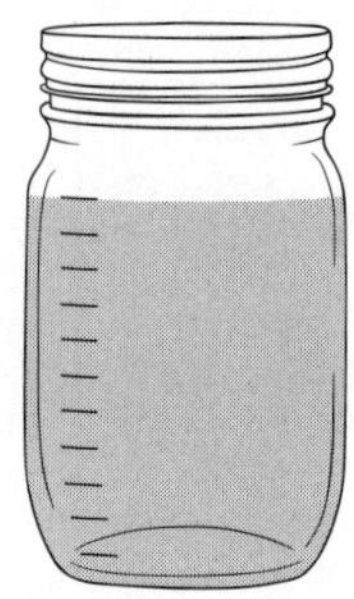	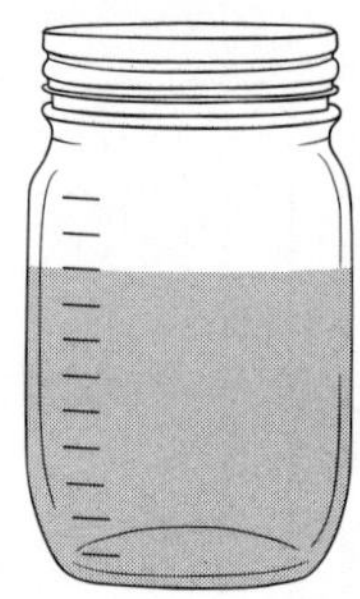	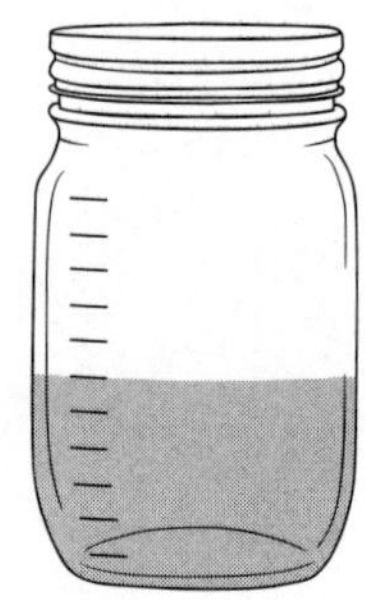

1. Which month had the most rainfall?

a. April

b. May

2. In May, there was __________ rain than in April.

a. more

b. less

3. What happened in March?

a. No rain fell.

b. It rained a lot.

Name: ______________________ **Date:** __________

Directions: Read the text. Answer the questions.

Bears hibernate in the winter. That means they sleep. There is little food to eat in the winter. In the spring, they wake up. Bears come out of their dens. They are hungry.

1. When do bears hibernate?

a. summer **b.** winter

2. Why do bears leave their dens in the spring?

a. to look for food **b.** to look for the sun

3. Say a question you have about bears hibernating.

Name: ______________________ **Date:** __________

Directions: Read the text. Answer the questions.

Carrie likes to play outside. Carrie likes to play outside in spring. In spring, the days get longer. In winter, the days are short.

1. What happens to the days in spring?

a. They get longer.

b. They get shorter.

2. When can Carrie play outside longer?

a. in the winter

b. in the spring

Name: ______________________________ **Date:** ____________

Directions: Color the things you could do in the spring.

Name: ______________________ Date: ____________

Directions: Read the text. Answer the questions.

Sizzling Summer

Summer comes after spring. Summer is the hottest season. The days are very long in the summer.

1. Which season is the hottest?

   a. summer

   b. spring

2. In the summer, the days are very ____________.

   a. long

   b. short

Name: ______________________________ **Date:** ____________

Directions: Look at the chart. Answer the questions.

Month	Amount of Sun	Number of Tomatoes
June	cloudy 	
July	partly cloudy 	
August	sunny 	

1. Which month was best for growing tomatoes?

a. August **b.** June

2. What do tomatoes need to grow?

a. lots of shade **b.** lots of sun

Name: ______________________ **Date:** __________

Directions: Read the text. Answer the questions.

Doreen likes butterflies. Doreen plants milkweed seeds. In summer, the seeds become flowers. Butterflies like milkweed flowers. They drink nectar from the flowers.

Developing Questions

1. What happens to milkweed seeds in the summer?

   a. They become flowers.

   b. They become butterflies.

2. What do butterflies like to drink?

   a. nectar

   b. seeds

3. Say a question you have about butterflies.

Name: ______________________ **Date:** __________

Directions: Read the text. Answer the questions.

Mai loves summer. Mai likes to play tennis. The sun is very hot. She wears sunscreen so she won't get burned by the sun.

1. What does Mai need to wear to not get burned?

a. sunscreen **b.** shorts

2. What else could Mai do to protect her from the sun?

a. play in the afternoon **b.** play indoors

3. What should Mai plan to wear to protect herself from the sun?

a.

b.

Communicating Results

Name: ______________________________ **Date:** ____________

Directions: Draw things you would bring to the beach in summer. Then, color the picture.

Name: ______________________________ **Date:** ____________

Directions: Read the text. Answer the questions.

Fall Features

Fall comes after summer. The days get shorter. The weather gets cooler. Leaves on trees may change color. Fall is also called autumn.

1. Fall comes after ______________.

a. summer **b.** winter

2. What happens to leaves in the fall?

a. They change color. **b.** They change shape.

3. What is another name for fall?

a. spring **b.** autumn

Name: ______________________________ **Date:** ____________

Directions: Fall comes after summer. Look at the chart. Answer the questions.

		Summer	Fall
hot weather		X	
cool weather			X
Halloween			X
long days		X	

1. In which season is Halloween?

a. fall **b.** summer

2. What is the weather like in the fall?

a. It is hot. **b.** It is cool.

Name: ______________________ **Date:** ____________

Directions: Read the text. Answer the questions.

Kanita has two trees in her yard. She has a maple tree and a magnolia tree. Maple trees lose their leaves in the fall. Magnolia trees keep their leaves all year long.

1. Which tree will lose its leaves in the fall?

a. maple tree

b. magnolia tree

2. Say a question about magnolia trees.

3. Say a question about maple trees.

Name: ______________________ **Date:** ____________

Directions: Read the text. Answer the questions.

Squirrels collect nuts in the fall. Squirrels eat the nuts in the winter. Kaz watches squirrels collect nuts and run away. In the winter, Kaz watches them eat the nuts.

1. Why do squirrels collect nuts in the fall?

a. to eat them in the winter

b. to build nests with them

2. How can Kaz find out where squirrels take their nuts?

a. He can hide the nuts.

b. He can follow the squirrels.

Name: ______________________ **Date:** __________

Directions: Maple trees change color in the fall. Magnolia trees stay green. Color the trees the way they would look in the fall.

Maple tree

Magnolia tree

Name: ______________________ **Date:** __________

Directions: Read the text. Answer the questions.

Land, Water, Air

We live on Earth. Earth is made up of land, water, and air. We walk on land. We swim in water. We breathe air.

1. Earth is made up of land, water, and __________.

   a. air **b.** cars

2. What do we do on land?

   a. walk

   b. swim

3. What do we do in water?

   a. swim

   b. cycle

Analyzing Data

Name: ______________________________ **Date:** ____________

Directions: Animals live in many places Look at the chart. Answer the questions.

	Land	**Air**	**Water**
		X	
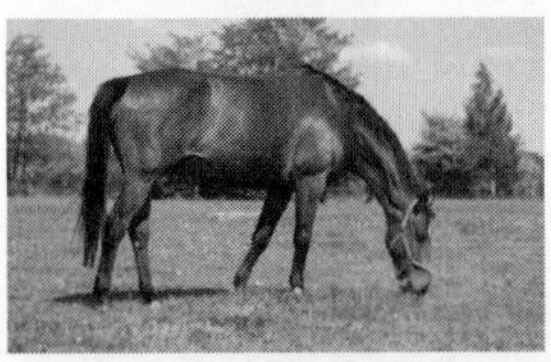	X		
			X

1. Where do horses live?

a. On the land. **b.** In the air.

2. Which animal lives in the air?

a. an eagle **b.** a fish

Name: ______________________ **Date:** __________

Directions: Read the text. Answer the questions.

Chet has a dog. The dog likes to dig in the dirt. The dog digs up many things.

1. What could Chet's dog dig up?

a. rocks

b. a fish

2. Say a question about things you find under the ground.

Name: ______________________ **Date:** ____________

Directions: Read the text. Answer the questions.

Air is everywhere. Air moves. We can see air move when a flag waves. We can feel air when it's windy outside.

1. How can you show your friend that air is everywhere?

   a. You can show a flag waving.

   b. You can show a car moving.

2. What could you do to feel air at home?

   a. You can sit in front of the TV.

   b. You can sit in front of a fan.

Communicating Results

ABC

Name: ______________________ **Date:** ____________

Directions: Draw an animal that lives on land. Draw an animal that flies in the air. Draw an animal that lives in water.

Land

Air

Water

Name: ______________________ Date: __________

Directions: Read the text. Answer the questions.

Desert, Tundras, and Savannas

Earth has deserts. Deserts are hot and dry. Earth has tundras. Tundras are cold and icy. Earth has savannas. Savannas have many animals like lions and giraffes.

1. Deserts are ______________.

   a. dry **b.** wet

2. What is in the tundra?

   a. ice

   b. grass

3. Where do lions live?

   a. In the tundra. **b.** In the savanna.

Name: ______________________ **Date:** ____________

Directions: Look at the chart. Answer the questions.

Desert	Tundra	Savanna
camel 	polar bear 	zebras 
rattlesnake 	penguins 	lions 

1. Which animal lives in the tundra?

   a. 

   b. 

2. Where can you find a zebra?

   a. desert

   b. savanna

3. Where does a camel live?

   a. desert

   b. tundra

Name: ______________________ **Date:** __________

Directions: Read the text. Answer the questions.

Camels live in the desert. Camels have thick eyebrows. They protect their eyes from the sun. Camels have thick lips so they can eat any plant.

1. What protects camels' eyes from the sun?
   - **a.** thick eyebrows
   - **b.** small eyes
2. Say a question you have about camels.
3. Say a question you have about living in the desert.

Name: ______________________ **Date:** __________

Directions: Read the text. Answer the questions.

Baby polar bears need to keep warm. Baby polar bears only have one coat of fur. Adult polar bears have two coats of fur. The snow den is where polar bears live. The snow den keeps adult and baby polar bears warm.

1. What could a baby polar bear do to keep warm?

a. play in the snow

b. stay close to its mother

2. What else could a polar bear do to keep warm?

a. splash around in the water

b. stay in their snow den

Name: ______________________ **Date:** ______________

Directions: Match each animal to its home.

giraffe

desert

penguin

tundra

rattlesnake

savanna

Name: ______________________ **Date:** __________

Directions: Read the text. Answer the questions.

From Rainforests to Oceans

Rainforests get lots of rain. It is very hot and wet. Oceans are full of water. On Earth, there is more water than land.

1. Rainforests get lots of ____________.

a. rain

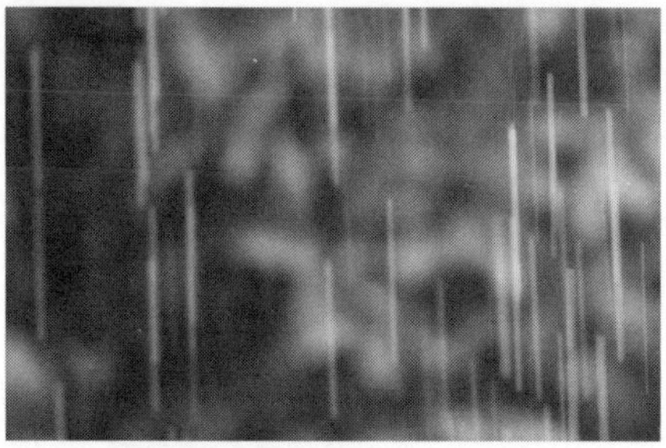

b. snow

2. What is the ocean made of?

a. water **b.** grass

3. Which is there more of on Earth?

a. land **b.** water

Name: ______________________ Date: ____________

Directions: Read the text. Look at the picture. Answer the questions.

The rainforest has layers. Different animals live in each layer.

1. Which animal lives in the lowest layer?

a.

b.

2. Where do squirrel monkeys live?

a. in the tree tops

b. on the ground

Name: ______________________ **Date:** ____________

Directions: Read the text. Answer the questions.

Oceans are big. They are bigger than lakes. Most lakes are made of freshwater. Oceans are made of saltwater.

1. Which is bigger?
   - **a.** oceans
   - **b.** lakes
2. What kind of water is in the ocean?
   - **a.** freshwater
   - **b.** saltwater
3. Say a question you have about oceans.

Name: ______________________ **Date:** ____________

Directions: Read the text. Answer the questions.

Lonny is going to hike in the rainforest. The rainforest is hot. It rains a lot in the rainforest. There are many bugs that bite.

1. What should Lonny pack for his trip?

a.

b.

2. What could Lonny do not to get bitten by bugs?

a. wear shorts and a T-shirt

b. put on bug spray

Name: ______________________________ **Date:** ____________

Directions: Read the text. Draw the animals in their ocean habitat.

The ocean is very deep. Sharks, dolphins, and turtles live near the top. Whales, octopuses, and crabs live farther down.

Name: ______________________ **Date:** __________

Directions: Read the text. Answer the questions.

The Sun, Moon, and Stars

The sun is in the sky. The moon and stars are in the sky, too. The sun gives Earth light and heat. The moon is smaller than Earth. Stars are very far away from Earth.

1. What does the sun give Earth?

   a. light b. rain

2. Which is smaller?

   a. Earth

   b. the moon

3. Stars are very __________.

   a. close b. far away

Analyzing Data

Name: ______________________________ **Date:** ____________

Directions: Look at the pictures of the sun. Answer the questions.

Morning	Noon	Evening

1. Which picture shows the sun in the morning?

a. 

b. 

2. Which picture shows the sun at noon?

a. 

b. 

Name: ____________________ **Date:** __________

Directions: Read the text. Look at the pictures. Answer the questions.

Every week Alice looks up at the moon. She sees four different shapes of the moon. When she can't see the moon, it's called a "new moon."

full moon

gibbous moon

first quarter moon

crescent moon

1. Alice sees a full moon. What does it look like?

a. 

b. 

2. What kind of moon can you **NOT** see?

a. old moon **b.** new moon

3. Say a question Alice could ask about the moon.

Name: ______________________ **Date:** __________

Directions: Read the text. Answer the questions.

Eddie looks at the sky. The sun looks big because the sun is close to Earth. The stars look small because they are far away.

1. Why does the sun look big?

a. It is far away. **b.** It is close to Earth.

2. Stars look small because __________ .

a. They are far away. **b.** They aren't bright.

3. What could Eddie do to see the stars up close?

a. use sunglasses

b. use a telescope

Name: ______________________ Date: __________

Directions: Match the picture with its description.

• This gives Earth light and heat.

• This object is smaller than Earth.

• These twinkle at night.

Learning Content

Name: ______________________ **Date:** ____________

Directions: Read the text. Answer the questions.

Earth

Earth is a planet. It is the planet we live on. Earth is made of rock and water.

1. What is the Earth?

   a. A planet.

   b. A sun.

2. Earth is made of rock and ____________.

   a. water

   b. planets

Name: ______________________________ **Date:** ______________

Directions: Read the text. Look at the photos. Answer the questions.

Earth is made of rock and water. We use rock and water in many ways.

Rock			
Water			

1. What is one way we use water?

   a. taking a shower **b.** riding a bike

2. What can we make out of rocks?

   a. a house **b.** cheese

Name: ______________________ **Date:** __________

Directions: Read the text. Look at the pictures. Answer the questions.

Dana takes a plane ride. Dana sees mountains. She sees hills. They rise high above the ground. Dana sees valley and flat plains, too.

1. What rises high above the Earth?

   a. mountains b. valleys

2. Which landform is flat?

   a. hills

   b. plains

3. Say a question Alice could have about mountains.

Name: ______________________________ Date: ____________

Directions: Read the text. Answer the questions.

Earth has many bodies of water. Bodies of water can be small like ponds and rivers. Bodies of water can be big, like lakes and oceans. Sam likes to swim in all of them.

1. An ocean is a ______________ body of water.

a. small **b.** large

2. If Sam wants to swim with dolphins, where should he swim?

a. pond

b. ocean

Name: ______________________ **Date:** ____________

Directions: Match the activity to the landform.

skiing

forest

fishing

mountain

hiking

river

Name: ______________________________ **Date:** ____________

Directions: Read the text. Answer the questions.

Taking Care of Earth

We take care of Earth in many ways. We put trash in bins. We recycle paper and plastic. We reuse bags and bottles. We walk and bike.

1. We take care of Earth by ______________.

a. recycling plastic bottles

b. throwing trash out the window

2. To help Earth, what could we do with an old plastic bag?

a. reuse it

b. throw it away

Analyzing Data

Name: ______________________________ **Date:** ____________

Directions: We get around in many ways. Look at the photos. Answer the questions.

Bad for Earth	Good for Earth

1. Which is a better for Earth?

a. driving a car

b. riding a bike

2. Jet skiing on the water is ____________.

a. good for Earth

b. bad for Earth

Name: ______________________________ **Date:** ____________

Directions: Read the text. Look at the picture. Answer the questions.

Reusing things is good. Reusing is good for Earth. Gentry has many coins. Gentry needs to put the coins in a jar.

1. What should Gentry do?

a. reuse an empty jar from her kitchen

b. buy a new jar from the store

2. Say a question about reusing things from home.

Name: ______________________ **Date:** ____________

Directions: Read the text. Answer the questions.

Mara washes dishes. Mara washes dishes every night. Then she takes a shower before bed. She knows that using less water is good for Earth.

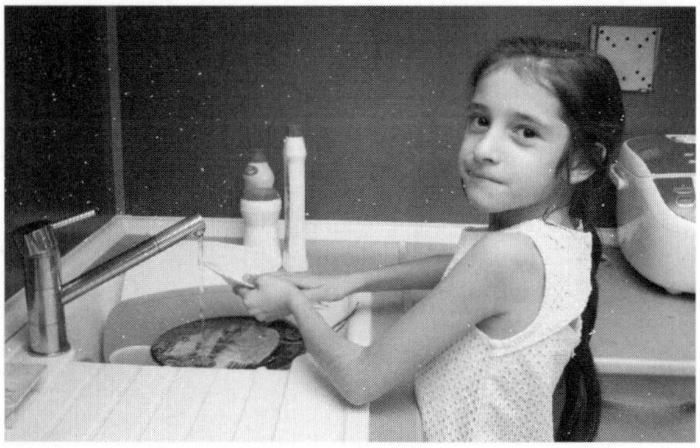

1. What should Mara do to help the Earth?

a. Use more water to wash the dishes.

b. Use less water to wash the dishes.

2. To help Earth, Mara should take a ______________.

a. long shower

b. short shower

3. How else could Mara use less water?

a. turn off the tap while brushing her teeth

b. turn on the tap while brushing her teeth

Name: ______________________ **Date:** __________

Directions: Circle the objects you can reuse.

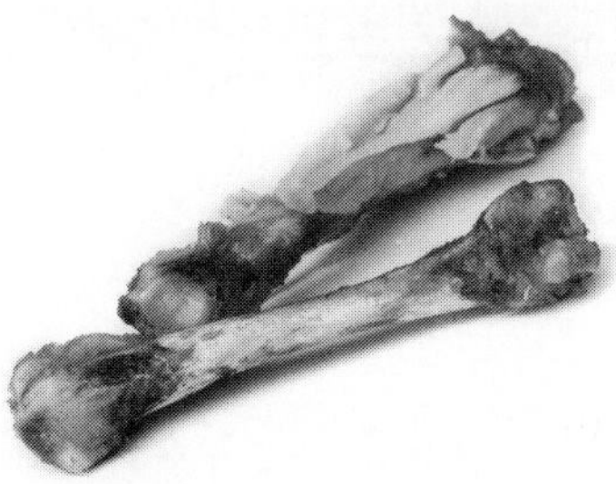

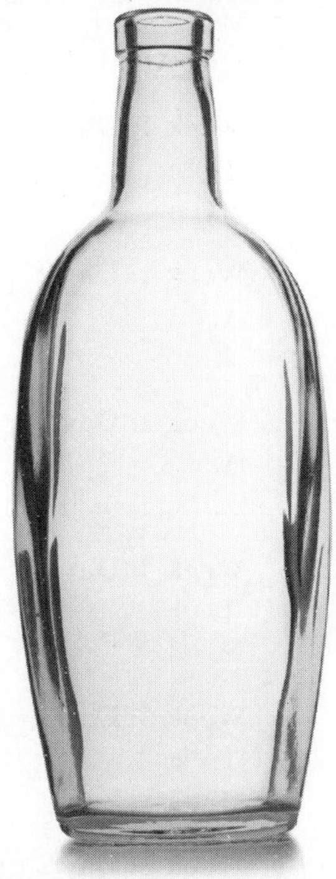

Answer Key

Life Science

Week 1: Day 1 (page 14)
1. a
2. a

Week 1: Day 2 (page 15)
1. a
2. a

Week 1: Day 3 (page 16)
1. b
2. a
3. Questions will vary.

Week 1: Day 4 (page 17)
1. b
2. Drawings will vary

Week 1: Day 5 (page 18)
1. wet food
2. wet food

Week 2: Day 1 (page 19)
1. a
2. a

Week 2: Day 2 (page 20)
1. b
2. a

Week 2: Day 3 (page 21)
1. a
2. Questions will vary.
3. Questions will vary.

Week 2: Day 4 (page 22)
1. a
2. a

Week 3: Day 1 (page 24)
1. a
2. a

Week 3: Day 2 (page 25)
1. a
2. a

Week 3: Day 3 (page 26)
1. a
2. Questions will vary.

Week 3: Day 4 (page 27)
1. a
2. a

Week 3: Day 5 (page 28)
My EYES help me see
My NOSE helps me smell
My EARS help me hear

Week 4: Day 1 (page 29)
1. a
2. a

Week 4: Day 2 (page 30)
1. a
2. b

Week 4: Day 3 (page 31)
1. a
2. Questions will vary.

Week 4: Day 4 (page 32)
1. b
2. a

Week 5: Day 1 (page 34)
1. a
2. a

Week 5: Day 2 (page 35)
1. a
2. a

Week 5: Day 3 (page 36)
1. b
2. Questions will vary.

Week 5: Day 4 (page 37)
1. a
2. a

Week 5: Day 5 (page 38)
From top to bottom: flower, leaves, stem, roots

Week 6: Day 1 (page 39)
1. b
2. b

Week 6: Day 2 (page 40)
1. a
2. a

Week 6: Day 3 (page 41)
1. a
2. b
3. b

Answer Key *(cont.)*

Week 6: Day 4 (page 42)

1. a
2. a
3. Answers will vary but may include water, sun, and soil.

Week 7: Day 1 (page 44)

1. b
2. a

Week 7: Day 2 (page 45)

1. b
2. a

Week 7: Day 3 (page 46)

1. b
2. b
3. Questions will vary.

Week 7: Day 4 (page 47)

1. b
2. a
3. a

Week 7: Day 5 (page 48)

Make sure the child draws six legs on the insect and eight legs on the arachnid.

Week 8: Day 1 (page 49)

1. b
2. a

Week 8: Day 2 (page 50)

1. b
2. a

Week 8: Day 3 (page 51)

1. a
2. Questions will vary.

Week 8: Day 4 (page 52)

1. b
2. Students can draw various things like fish or grass.

Week 8: Day 5 (page 53)

earthworm—underground
camel—desert
dolphin—ocean
deer—forest

Week 9: Day 1 (page 54)

1. b
2. a

Week 9: Day 2 (page 55)

1. a
2. b

Week 9: Day 3 (page 56)

1. a
2. Questions will vary.

Week 9: Day 4 (page 57)

1. b
2. a
3. a

Week 9: Day 5 (page 58)

Make sure students include the items in the box in their drawing.

Week 10: Day 1 (page 59)

1. a
2. b
3. b

Week 10: Day 2 (page 60)

1. a
2. b
3. a

Week 10: Day 3 (page 61)

1. a
2. b
3. Questions will vary.

Week 10: Day 4 (page 62)

1. a
2. b
3. Students should draw a baby animal and its parent.

Week 10: Day 5 (page 63)

frog—tadpole
dog—puppy
kangaroo—joey
chicken—chick

Week 11: Day 1 (page 64)

1. b
2. b

Week 11: Day 2 (page 65)

1. a
2. b
3. b

Week 11: Day 3 (page 66)

1. a
2. Questions will vary.
3. Questions will vary.

Answer Key *(cont.)*

Week 11: Day 4 (page 67)
1. b
2. a

Week 12: Day 1 (page 69)
1. b
2. b

Week 12: Day 2 (page 70)
1. b
2. a

Week 12: Day 3 (page 71)
1. b
2. a
3. Questions will vary.
4. Questions will vary.

Week 12: Day 4 (page 72)
1. a
2. Answers will vary, but make sure the food students draw is a healthy food.

Physical Science

Week 1: Day 1 (page 74)
1. b
2. b

Week 1: Day 2 (page 75)
1. b
2. a

Week 1: Day 3 (page 76)
1. a
2. b
3. Questions will vary.

Week 1: Day 4 (page 77)
1. a
2. a

Week 1: Day 5 (page 78)
Pictures will vary.

Week 2: Day 1 (page 79)
1. a
2. b

Week 2: Day 2 (page 80)
1. a
2. a

Week 2: Day 3 (page 81)
1. a
2. Questions will vary.

Week 2: Day 4 (page 82)
1. a
2. a

Week 2: Day 5 (page 83)
Pictures will vary.

Week 3: Day 1 (page 84)
1. a
2. b

Week 3: Day 2 (page 85)
1. b
2. a

Week 3: Day 3 (page 86)
1. a
2. a
3. Questions will vary.

Week 3: Day 4 (page 87)
1. a
2. b
3. a

Week 3: Day 5 (page 88)
Pictures will vary.

Week 4: Day 1 (page 89)
1. b
2. b

Week 4: Day 2 (page 90)
1. b
2. a

Week 4: Day 3 (page 91)
1. a
2. b
3. Questions will vary.

Week 4: Day 4 (page 92)
1. b
2. a
3. a

Week 4: Day 5 (page 93)
Color—flying bird; flying plane
Trace—bird in water; plane on ground

Answer Key *(cont.)*

Week 5: Day 1 (page 94)
1. b
2. b

Week 5: Day 2 (page 95)
1. a
2. b

Week 5: Day 3 (page 96)
1. a
2. b
3. Questions will vary.

Week 5: Day 4 (page 97)
1. b
2. a

Week 5: Day 5 (page 98)
Magnetic objects are the fork, keys, safety pin, and paper clip.

Week 6: Day 1 (page 99)
1. b
2. b

Week 6: Day 2 (page 100)
1. a
2. a
3. a

Week 6: Day 3 (page 101)
1. b
2. a
3. Questions will vary.

Week 6: Day 4 (page 102)
1. a
2. a
3. b

Week 7: Day 1 (page 104)
1. a
2. a
3. b

Week 7: Day 2 (page 105)
1. a
2. a

Week 7: Day 3 (page 106)
1. a
2. b
3. Questions will vary.

Week 7: Day 4 (page 107)
1. a
2. a
3. a

Week 7: Day 5 (page 108)
The clothes of the girl on the swing should be colored red. The clothes of the boy behind the fence should be colored blue.

Week 8: Day 1 (page 109)
1. a
2. b

Week 8: Day 2 (page 110)
1. a
2. a

Week 8: Day 3 (page 111)
1. a
2. a
3. a

Week 8: Day 4 (page 112)
1. b
2. a
3. a

Week 8: Day 5 (page 113)
Pictures will vary.

Week 9: Day 1 (page 114)
1. a
2. b

Week 9: Day 2 (page 115)
1. a
2. b

Week 9: Day 3 (page 116)
1. a
2. a
3. Questions will vary.

Week 9: Day 4 (page 117)
1. a
2. b

Week 9: Day 5 (page 118)
Pictures will vary.

Week 10: Day 1 (page 119)
1. a
2. b

Answer Key *(cont.)*

Week 10: Day 2 (page 120)
1. a
2. a

Week 10: Day 3 (page 121)
1. a
2. b
3. Questions will vary.

Week 10: Day 4 (page 122)
1. a
2. a
3. b

Week 10: Day 5 (page 123)
Pictures will vary.

Week 11: Day 1 (page 124)
1. a
2. a

Week 11: Day 2 (page 125)
1. a
2. b

Week 11: Day 3 (page 126)
1. a
2. a
3. Questions will vary.

Week 11: Day 4 (page 127)
1. a
2. a
3. b

Week 11: Day 5 (page 128)
Green/brown—mountains, trees, grass, wood, rocks
Blue—water
Yellow—clouds, smoke

Week 12: Day 1 (page 129)
1. a
2. a

Week 12: Day 2 (page 130)
1. a
2. a

Week 12: Day 3 (page 131)
1. a
2. a
3. Questions will vary.

Week 12: Day 4 (page 132)
1. a
2. b

Week 12: Day 5 (page 133)
Red (toys)—firetruck, soccer ball, teddy bear, skateboard
Blue (tools)—magnifying glass, measuring cup, globe, clock, thermometer, binoculars

Earth and Space Science

Week 1: Day 1 (page 134)
1. a
2. b

Week 1: Day 2 (page 135)
1. a
2. b

Week 1: Day 3 (page 136)
1. a
2. a
3. Questions will vary.

Week 1: Day 4 (page 137)
1. a
2. a
3. a

Week 1: Day 5 (page 138)
Pictures will vary.

Week 2: Day 1 (page 139)
1. a
2. a

Week 2: Day 2 (page 140)
1. a
2. b
3. a

Week 2: Day 3 (page 141)
1. a
2. Questions will vary.
3. Questions will vary.

Week 2: Day 4 (page 142)
1. b
2. a

Week 2: Day 5 (page 143)
Winter—skiing
Spring—plant a garden
Summer—swimming
Fall—picking pumpkins

Answer Key *(cont.)*

Week 3: Day 1 (page 144)

1. a
2. a
3. a

Week 3: Day 2 (page 145)

1. a
2. b
3. a

Week 3: Day 3 (page 146)

1. a
2. a
3. Questions will vary.

Week 3: Day 4 (page 147)

1. a
2. b

Week 4: Day 1 (page 149)

1. a
2. a
3. a

Week 4: Day 2 (page 150)

1. a
2. b
3. a

Week 4: Day 3 (page 151)

1. b
2. a
3. Questions will vary.

Week 4: Day 4 (page 152)

1. a
2. b

Week 5: Day 1 (page 154)

1. a
2. a

Week 5: Day 2 (page 155)

1. a
2. b

Week 5: Day 3 (page 156)

1. a
2. a
3. Questions will vary.

Week 5: Day 4 (page 157)

1. a
2. b
3. a

Week 5: Day 5 (page 158)

Pictures will vary.

Week 6: Day 1 (page 159)

1. a
2. a
3. b

Week 6: Day 2 (page 160)

1. a
2. b

Week 6: Day 3 (page 161)

1. a
2. Questions will vary.
3. Questions will vary.

Week 6: Day 4 (page 162)

1. a
2. b
3. Questions will vary.

Week 6: Day 5 (page 163)

The maple tree should look barren. The magnolia tree should look full.

Week 7: Day 1 (page 164)

1. a
2. a
3. a

Week 7: Day 2 (page 165)

1. a
2. a

Week 7: Day 3 (page 166)

1. a
2. Questions will vary.

Week 7: Day 4 (page 167)

1. a
2. b

Week 8: Day 1 (page 169)

1. a
2. a
3. b

Week 8: Day 2 (page 170)

1. a
2. b
3. a

Answer Key *(cont.)*

Week 8: Day 3 (page 171)
1. a
2. Questions will vary.
3. Questions will vary.

Week 8: Day 4 (page 172)
1. b
2. b

Week 8: Day 5 (page 173)
Giraffe—savanna
Penguin—tundra
Rattlesnake—desert

Week 9: Day 1 (page 174)
1. a
2. a
3. b

Week 9: Day 2 (page 175)
1. a
2. a

Week 9: Day 3 (page 176)
1. a
2. b
3. Questions will vary.

Week 9: Day 4 (page 177)
1. b
2. b

Week 10: Day 1 (page 179)
1. a
2. b
3. b

Week 10: Day 2 (page 180)
1. a
2. b

Week 10: Day 3 (page 181)
1. a
2. b
3. Questions will vary.

Week 10: Day 4 (page 182)
1. b
2. a
3. b

Week 10: Day 5 (page 183)
Stars—"These twinkle at night."
Sun—"This gives Earth light and heat."
Moon—"This object is smaller than Earth."

Week 11: Day 1 (page 184)
1. a
2. a

Week 11: Day 2 (page 185)
1. a
2. a

Week 11: Day 3 (page 186)
1. a
2. b
3. Questions will vary.

Week 11: Day 4 (page 187)
1. b
2. b

Week 11: Day 5 (page 188)
Skiing—mountain
Fishing—river
Hiking—forest

Week 12: Day 1 (page 189)
1. a
2. a

Week 12: Day 2 (page 190)
1. b
2. b

Week 12: Day 3 (page 191)
1. a
2. Questions will vary.

Week 12: Day 4 (page 192)
1. b
2. b
3. a

Week 12: Day 5 (page 193)
Circled items should be glass bottle, jar, plastic bottle, and paper bag.

Notes

Student Name: ______________________ **Date:** ______________

Developing Questions Rubric

Directions: Complete this rubric every four weeks to evaluate students' Day 3 activity sheets. Only one rubric is needed per student. Their work over the four weeks can be evaluated together. Evaluate their work in each category by writing a score in each row. Then, add up their scores, and write the total on the line. Students may earn up to 5 points in each row and up to 15 points total.

Skill	5	3	1	Score
Asking Scientific Questions	Asks scientific questions related to text all or nearly all the time.	Asks scientific questions related to text most of the time.	Does not ask scientific questions related to text.	
Interpreting Text	Correctly interprets texts to answer questions all or nearly all the time.	Correctly interprets texts to answer questions most of the time.	Does not correctly interpret texts to answer questions.	
Applying Information	Applies new information to form questions all or nearly all the time.	Applies new information to form questions most of the time.	Does not apply new information to form questions.	

Total Points: ____________

Student Name: ______________________ **Date:** ____________

Planning Solutions Rubric

Directions: Complete this rubric every four weeks to evaluate students' Day 4 activity sheets. Only one rubric is needed per student. Their work over the four weeks can be evaluated together. Evaluate their work in each category by writing a score in each row. Then, add up their scores, and write the total on the line. Students may earn up to 5 points in each row and up to 15 points total.

Skill	5	3	1	Score
Planning Tests	Plans reasonable tests to study topics all or nearly all the time.	Plans reasonable tests to study topics most of the time.	Does not plan reasonable tests to study topics.	
Making Predictions	Makes reasonable predictions all or nearly all the time.	Makes reasonable predictions most of the time.	Does not make reasonable predictions.	
Choosing Next Steps	Chooses reasonable next steps for tests all or nearly all the time.	Chooses reasonable next steps for tests most of the time.	Does not choose reasonable next steps for tests.	

Total Points: ____________

Student Name: ______________________ **Date:** ____________

Communicating Results Rubric

Directions: Complete this rubric every four weeks to evaluate students' Day 5 activity sheets. Only one rubric is needed per student. Their work over the four weeks can be evaluated together. Evaluate their work in each category by writing a score in each row. Then, add up their scores, and write the total on the line. Students may earn up to 5 points in each row and up to 15 points total.

Skill	5	3	1	Score
Showing Data	Creates charts and graphs to correctly show data all or nearly all the time.	Creates charts and graphs to correctly show data most of the time.	Does not create charts and graphs to correctly show data.	
Making Connections	Makes connections between new information and prior knowledge all or nearly all the time.	Makes connections between new information and prior knowledge most of the time.	Does not make connections between new information and prior knowledge.	
Explaining Results	Uses evidence to explain results all or nearly all the time.	Uses evidence to explain results most of the time.	Does not use evidence to explain results.	

Total Points: ____________

Life Science Analysis Chart

Directions: Record the total of each student's Day 1 and Day 2 scores from the four weeks. Then, record each student's rubric scores (pages 202–204). Add the totals, and record the sums in the Total Scores column. Record the average class score in the last row.

Student Name	Week 4					Week 8					Week 12					Total Scores
	Day 1	Day 2	DQ	PS	CR	Day 1	Day 2	DQ	PS	CR	Day 1	Day 2	DQ	PS	CR	
Average Classroom Score																

DQ = Developing Questions, PS = Planning Solutions, CR = Communicating Results

Physical Science Analysis Chart

Directions: Record the total of each student's Day 1 and Day 2 scores from the four weeks. Then, record each student's rubric scores (pages 202–204). Add the totals, and record the sums in the Total Scores column. Record the average class score in the last row.

Student Name	Week 4					Week 8					Week 12					Total Scores
	Day 1	Day 2	DQ	PS	CR	Day 1	Day 2	DQ	PS	CR	Day 1	Day 2	DQ	PS	CR	
Average Classroom Score																

DQ = Developing Questions, PS = Planning Solutions, CR = Communicating Results

Earth and Space Science Analysis Chart

Directions: Record the total of each student's Day 1 and Day 2 scores from the four weeks. Then, record each student's rubric scores (pages 202–204). Add the totals, and record the sums in the Total Scores column. Record the average class score in the last row.

Student Name	Week 4					Week 8					Week 12					Total Scores
	Day 1	Day 2	DQ	PS	CR	Day 1	Day 2	DQ	PS	CR	Day 1	Day 2	DQ	PS	CR	
Average Classroom Score																

DQ = Developing Questions, PS = Planning Solutions, CR = Communicating Results

Digital Resources

To access digital resources, go to this website and enter the following code: 89319049
www.teachercreatedmaterials.com/administrators/download-files/

Rubrics

Resource	Filename
Developing Questions Rubric	questionsrubric.pdf
Planning Solutions Rubric	solutionsrubric.pdf
Communicating Results Rubric	resultsrubric.pdf

Item Analysis Sheets

Resource	Filename
Life Science Analysis Chart	LSanalysischart.pdf LSanalysischart.docx LSanalysischart.xlsx
Physical Science Analysis Chart	PSanalysischart.pdf PSanalysischart.docx PSanalysischart.xlsx
Earth and Space Science Analysis Chart	ESSanalysischart.pdf ESSanalysischart.docx ESSanalysischart.xlsx

Standards

Resource	Filename
Standards Charts	standards.pdf